Kasey Chambers is an Australian country music artist whose distinctive voice, heart-felt lyrics and world-class performances have earned her the rightful position as one of the most popular and acclaimed artists of her generation at home, while winning her a devoted cult following in the rest of the world. Hailed as bringing Australian country music into the mainstream, Kasey has won fourteen ARIA awards, twenty-four CMAA Golden Guitars and ten APRAs. Her twelve albums have sold more than fourteen times platinum. In 2018, she became the youngest woman ever to be inducted into the ARIA Hall of Fame. Now forty-eight years old, Kasey has three children, Talon, twenty-two, Arlo, seventeen, and Poet, twelve, and she lives on the central coast of New South Wales. She still writes songs, makes albums and travels playing music all around Australia with her partner, Brando, and dog, Buddy.

KASEY CHAMBERS

Just Don't Be a D**khead

AND OTHER PROFOUND THINGS I'VE LEARNT

Hardie Grant
BOOKS

Aboriginal and Torres Strait Islander Peoples are advised that this publication may contain the names and images of deceased people. Hardie Grant apologises for any distress this may inadvertently cause.

Published in 2024 by Hardie Grant Books,
an imprint of Hardie Grant Publishing

Hardie Grant Books (Melbourne)
Wurundjeri Country
Building 1, 658 Church Street
Richmond, Victoria 3121

Hardie Grant North America
2912 Telegraph Ave
Berkeley, California 94705

hardiegrant.com/books

Hardie Grant acknowledges the Traditional Owners of the Country on which we work, the Wurundjeri People of the Kulin Nation and the Gadigal People of the Eora Nation, and recognises their continuing connection to the land, waters and culture. We pay our respects to their Elders past and present.

NATIONAL LIBRARY OF AUSTRALIA
A catalogue record for this book is available from the National Library of Australia

Just Don't Be a Dickhead
ISBN 978 1 76145 102 7
ISBN 978 1 76144 231 5 (ebook)

10 9 8 7 6 5 4 3 2 1
Publishing Director: Pam Brewster
Head of Editorial: Jasmin Chua
Project Editor: Claire Davis
Editor: Kimberley Davis
Design Manager: Kristin Thomas
Cover Design: Kate Barraclough
Typesetter: Kate Barraclough
Head of Production: Todd Rechner
Production Controller: Jessica Harvie

Printed in Canada

FSC www.fsc.org MIX Paper | Supporting responsible forestry FSC® C016245

The paper this book is printed on is certified against the Forest Stewardship Council® Standards. Griffin Press holds FSC® chain of custody certification SCS-COC-001185. FSC® promotes environmentally responsible, socially beneficial and economically viable management of the world's forests.

Contents

Foreword

It's an Aussie thing … it's a rural outback thing … and it's sure as shit a Chambers thing … This born-of-the-dirt, think-on-your-feet, no-bullshit way of being that not only helps you navigate life, but informs how you treat others as well.

I met Bill, Diane, Nash and 'little' Kasey sometime in the late '80s. I loved them immediately – because they were REAL PEOPLE. You knew it right away. Kasey, man, even as a young teenager, was already full of fire, charisma and mystic earthiness. Over the years I've watched her blossom into this extraordinary artist, singer, songwriter, storyteller, Aussie icon. (Not coincidentally with Nash at the helm producing her records, and Bill and Diane always in the mix.)

Personally, I'm grateful that Kasey decided not only to write this book, but to publish it as well. I find myself today hearing my own mum and dad's little tidbits, sayings and expressions that resonate in 'Aha!' ways all the time.

I also feel, in so many ways, we've lost a lot of the ancient, tribal structures through which wisdom, experience and guidance are passed down to us. We don't even seem to seek them out, and yet we're totally flailing around without them. Sometimes it's the simplest truisms that light the way. Who knows, maybe there was an eleventh commandment and it simply stated: JUST DON'T BE A DICKHEAD.

KEITH URBAN

A note on intention

A little while before I finished writing this book, I started doubting whether I would release it anymore. There were two main reasons.

First, there were a few chapters that made me feel pretty uncomfortable. Opening up so much about some deep, honest things, and then putting that out there for anyone to read, was a bit confronting. I've obviously always put a lot of honesty and real feelings into my songs and put them out there, but this felt very different. A little more exposing, I guess. No production, instruments or band to hide behind. It felt more open. More candid. More raw.

Don't get me wrong, it's not like I've revealed every little secret I've ever had in this book or anything. There are still a few things I've kept to myself (like being an accomplice to the theft of a giant chicken sculpture from backstage at a well-known music festival, or a relatively serious shoe-shopping addiction that I'm not yet ready to dig into, or the unidentified rash that keeps returning that I'd rather not talk about) but I still felt quite vulnerable and open.

The other reason was that I'd started feeling a lot of self-doubt and embarrassment about the way that I write. I know I don't write like an actual author. I know I don't share my stories like professional writers with brilliant, well-informed, intelligent words and sentences carefully crafted to sound artistic and poetic. I mean, fuck. I ain't no Shakespeare. All of this is just in my words. Written by me, on my own. Not much to hide behind there. OK, maybe I hide behind a fair bit of humour, celebrity name-dropping and some shameless self-promotion (my new album, *Backbone*, is out now by the way), but that still isn't quite enough to completely cover up some of the hard truths and poor grammar that I've uncovered for myself.

So I was doubting whether I would release this book anymore at all. And I guess that felt OK. Just writing most of it had already been a journey in itself, mostly a beautiful walk down memory lane, with some laughter and tears, some extreme-gratitude reminders of so many amazing things in my life, some painful realities that felt clearer just from writing them down, some new lessons learnt, and some blunt realisations of how much I'm still not tuning into my 'inner foghorn' as much as I think I am. (Don't worry, you'll meet her soon.)

So I chatted to my friend Danni, and told her that as I got closer to finishing the book I was having a lot of doubtful days creeping in. And she said it's on those days that it's actually probably more important than ever to remind yourself of your true intention.

The truth is, my original intention for writing this book was never really about anyone else reading it. I began it one day by writing a list on my phone of the most important stuff I've learnt from my experiences in my life, and from inspiring and unlikely people I've crossed paths with. A list that I could read over again each day, and use to remind myself to at least try to live by these lessons as best I could. I thought I would end up with about ten.

But they just kept coming. More and more lessons. More and more things that I wanted to remind myself to live by every day. And then each lesson felt like a stepping stone that led to a story of an experience I'd had along the way, so I would write that down too. These words just kept coming. Something had swept me up, and I think that my higher old mate and my inner foghorn had taken over. Not in any kind of order. Just mostly word vomit pouring out.

Many years ago as I was creating my first solo album, *The Captain*, something was telling me that I was ready to share my songs with the world. That same feeling swept over me as I was writing these lessons and stories. It was naturally becoming a little book. (The entire thing ended up all being written in the Notes app on my phone.) A book that I felt like I now 'wanted' to share with other people, just like I share my songs. Not for any real reason or payoff. Just to share. Not everyone will like it, find it interesting, agree with it, care about it, wanna read it or get a thing from it, but sharing doesn't have to be about getting something back. Putting your real self out there is a liberating reward in itself. This book is just full of stuff that has helped shape who I am. Good things. Bad things. Inspiring things. Funny things. Hard things. Sad things. Joyful things. Uncomfortable things. Real things.

So I just kept writing. And writing. As I did, I started realising that, as well as matching up with inspiration for my old songs written over the years, so many of these lessons, stories and moments were also matching up with the inspiration for all the new songs – the ones that I had written in the last seven years since my last full-band solo album. The songs were bringing the book to life, and the book was bringing my songs to life. A new album was being born at the same time. *Backbone.* So I just kept writing.

But with that writing, with that creativity, with the birth of a new album, with the humour, the joyful memories and the open heart also came the awkward feelings, the realisation of my unprofessional writing style, and the uncomfortable honesty which then, of course, turned into more self-doubt, fear and anxiety. So I went back to that first list, my original intention, and I read the things on the list. I read them again. And again.

The last one on my list said 'Be brave enough to be vulnerable'. So I went back to the chapter where I talk about writing the song 'Not Pretty Enough'. Then I sat down in exactly the same spot where I created that list, and I decided that all I needed to do was finish the book with an open heart. I didn't ever actually have to share it with another person if I didn't want to. Just finish it now, and decide that later. Don't write for the listener or the reader – just write for the song. Write from who I am, not from who I want people to see me as.

Write from my heart.

My little inner foghorn popped up, and she reminded me that it's OK to just be vulnerable. Be real.

Everything's gonna be alright.

As for my self-doubt attached to my un-author-like writing style, I reminded myself of when I was struggling to prepare my speech for my induction into the ARIA Hall of Fame a few years back. I laboured over this speech for months and months, wondering why I, the most talkative, outspoken chatterbox in the world, who would talk the leg off a chair, couldn't fucking come up with anything profound to say for the most important moment of my career. I watched other artists' speeches, I read renowned poetry and lyrics looking for inspiring quotes and verses, but nothing felt quite right. This little voice deep inside me kept popping up. Maybe not classically appropriate, but my dad's advice over the years of 'Just don't be a dickhead' kept ringing in my ears and asking to be included – obviously not because it was profound. Not because it was deep or inspirational. But because it was just real. It meant something to me. And I truly believed it was good advice. I threw out all my other drafts, started again, and 'Just don't be a dickhead' became the glue that held my whole speech together. And it's something I genuinely try to live by.

I finished the book, and never really questioned whether I would share it again.

I truly believe that the more we can show on the outside of who we really are on the inside, warts and all, the more that other people might feel like they can do the same.

Less bullshit. More inner foghorn. And she always says to me, 'Just be you. Be real. Oh and … just don't be a dickhead.'

Everything's gonna be alright.

Throughout this book, every now and then, you'll find a QR code that leads you to a song from my album *Backbone* that's closely related to or inspired by the story you just read, if you wanna have a listen. If not, just ignore and keep reading!

'A NEW DAY HAS COME'

Prologue

It is April 1976, and my mum is seven months pregnant with me. My dad is a professional fox hunter. My brother, Nash, is almost three years old. We are all in my dad's old left-hand-drive army jeep, and it is late at night.

At this time, it's frequent for farmers in outback South Australia to hire hunters to keep the foxes away from their farm stock, but Dad – being the slightly unorthodox fellow he is – is hunting this one time (OK, probably not the only time) well after midnight, on a private property, without any permission. Hunting illegally like this is (from what I now understand) fairly common in the hunting community at this time, and if you mostly keep away from the farm homesteads, the shearing quarters and any domestic living areas, and stick to the property outskirts, you'll probably go unnoticed. Which my dad is under the impression he is doing. (Or so he says.) He whistles up a fox, and when in range he lines his sight up in the scope, pulls back the bolt on the high-powered rifle, breathes in and squeezes the trigger until it fires. Maybe with a little bit of help (and irony) from divine intervention, he misses the fox. The shot rings out loudly with a piercing echo through the dark, once-silent, thought-to-be-isolated bushland.

Then a light comes on out of nowhere.

The homestead! It's close. Really close. Right near where my dad is parked. Uh-oh.

An angry man comes bursting out of the verandah door. He's in just his undies, and he's holding a shotgun, eager to catch the intruders who have interrupted his slumber with their reckless behaviour. He runs towards our family jeep, yelling and waving his fist on one side and the shotgun on the other.

With no time to think clearly, my dad puts the jeep in drive, and yells 'Hang on tight!' to my pregnant mum. My brother, who is sleeping, wakes up suddenly, startled by all the commotion. Dad slams his foot down on the accelerator, and takes off in a cloud of dust. There are no seatbelts in jeeps in these days, so my mum grasps her unbuckled three-year-old child as tightly as only a protective mother can. His wide little eyes watch out the back window as the homestead light and the outraged farmer trail off into the distance and the darkness.

Phew. That was close.

As Dad's nerves calm a little, he lets out a sigh and takes the pressure off the accelerator. For a few seconds, he's relieved, thinking he's in the clear, when the double glow of a set of headlights appears in the rear-view mirror. Shit.

The displeased homestead owner is not letting his trespassers get away that easily. The headlights grow bigger as he shortens the stretch of rough and rocky road between his farm ute and our jeep.

OK, my dad thinks. *I reckon this guy is in a Holden ute, so he isn't likely to have much of a chance speed-wise against my jeep. We should be fine.*

His heart rate is still high, but he feels confident that he will outrun the farmer in no time. He puts the accelerator back down with the self-certainty that only someone who has been in a similar situation before could possibly have, and for the second time in less than a minute he watches the farmer disappear into the darkness.

His heart rate steady now, Dad composes himself, gives Mum a reassuring look (which I imagine probably meant nothing to her at this point), and continues his getaway. But suddenly the sound of his ever-faithful jeep is different. It's skipping. The hum of the engine is no longer smooth or steady; it's broken and uneven. The power drops. Dad looks down at the fuel gauge and sees the needle bouncing well below empty. Fuck.

We are running out of fuel.

Now I'm sure that, at this point, my dad is probably thinking there could not be a worse sound than his jeep spluttering as it tries to catch the last fumes of fuel from the tank, when the sudden sound of gunfire from behind proves him wrong. The farmer is firing towards us and, although he's still a long way behind, he's gaining on us by the second as the jeep slows down.

Dad chooses to think fast instead of clear, and hatches a plan that – although maybe a tad questionable in hindsight – could be the split-second difference between life and death (or jail time). With his foot still firmly on the accelerator, forcing the struggling little jeep to maintain as much forward movement as it can muster, he turns to my mum and says with urgency, 'Diane, there's a jerry can of fuel behind this seat and a hose next to it. I need you to quickly siphon fuel into the tank.'

I can only imagine that, when she hears this unusual request, my mum must be, somewhere in her mind, cursing my dad for getting her family into this kind of situation. She's maybe even wondering if she's actually picked the right life partner. But there's no one more capable or powerful than a mother protecting her son and unborn child from immediate gunfire, so she doesn't hesitate. She opens the jerry-can lid and quickly puts the hose in, then opens the window closest to the fuel-tank cap on the outside of the jeep and – seven months pregnant – she starts sucking on the other end of the hose to draw the fuel to the top.

The jeep is swerving and jerking around as my dad steers it over the bumpy, rugged road, but each turn allows the engine to kick back in with the change of balance in the fuel tank between misses. All the while, the farmer is drawing closer to us, with one hand on his steering wheel and the other on his shotgun, which is pointed and firing towards us out the window.

My mum keeps sucking on the hose, knowing it takes a few tries and some very big breaths to draw fuel up to the other end. Then, finally, with every bit of strength in her lungs, she manages to get the petrol flowing. She tries not to swallow the entire mouthful of petrol as it spurts up (which I'm sure I unconsciously appreciate from her womb), then she squeezes half of her unusually large body out of the open window and sticks the hose into the outside fuel-tank pipe. Now, her most important role is to hold that hose in place while the tank guzzles the fuel, so that her husband's reckless driving doesn't knock it out of the vehicle. She keeps one hand tightly on the hose, and rests the other on the edge of the window to hold her big-bellied body firmly in place on the outside of the vehicle and make sure she doesn't fall out of the jeep.

But is it too late?

The Holden ute is getting closer, and this must all be quite a sight for the farmer. In the glow of his headlights, he has full view of this chaotic scene as he gains on the jeep.

Inside the jeep, my brother is in shock. He isn't really able to comprehend the scenario going on around him, and is saying nothing in words but everything in the look on his face. And, as the jeep slows to a snail's pace, my dad is preparing for defeat. Has his plan failed? Is this where it all ends?

Then, just when all seems lost, the engine catches the fuel that my mum has successfully siphoned, and the faithful jeep kicks back in. The power returns with a force so strong and a timing so perfect that it could only have been created by the help of something far greater and unexplainable.

Foot to the floor, my dad leaves the exasperated farmer in his dust for the third and final time. Our family is out of harm's way.

More than willing to admit who the real hero is in this hard-to-believe but true story, my dad, Bill Chambers, will later sheepishly share the memory of the time back in 1976 that he was clearly a dickhead.

I was born two months later.

Always read the epilogue.

1.

Just don't be a dickhead

My dad's always been a simple, down-home, say-it-like-it-is kinda guy. Not exactly what you would call a philosophical, motivational-speaker type. Don't get me wrong, he's always had very strong beliefs, opinions, sense of faith, thoughts, morals and points of view, but he's never really needed for everyone to hear them or agree with him. He just lives his life his own way, choosing his own path, while letting others have theirs. If anyone was ever to go to him for guidance on life choices, or inspiration on how to take the next step into their future, I'm not sure they would ever get much more advice from him than: 'Just don't be a dickhead.'

Throughout my life, I've often heard my dad muttering those words. Both quietly, mumbled under his breath to others, and sometimes specifically directed at my brother and me when we'd done something stupid. It was never offensive, or taken very seriously, as we would usually just laugh at him and continue our stupid behaviour.

So, having heard this phrase so many times over the years, I can't really look back and find some lightbulb moment or awakening when it changed my life or anything. But eventually, as the years have gone by, these subtly disguised words of wisdom have popped into my mind more and more, and when I least expect it. Sometimes when I've been faced with important and poignant life choices.

'Just don't be a dickhead.'

I know the wording isn't exactly profound, and some would say the general definition of 'being a dickhead' is arguably up for debate, but the older I've gotten the more I think I've started to understand the message behind my dad's true intention. Simple. Straight to the point. And something we might all need to hear from time to time.

It certainly does cover a lot of things that I'd like to live by. I've even started to think it could (and probably should) be tagged onto the end of every piece of advice I've ever tried to give myself:

'Be yourself, stand up for yourself, have a mind of your own … and just don't be a dickhead.'

'Say what you truly think and feel, and be as honest as you can … and just don't be a dickhead.'

'Make your own choices based on what is right for you … but just don't be a dickhead.'

'Lead with love and kindness … and just don't be a dickhead.'

'Have strong beliefs and opinions, and disagree with people if you need to … but just don't be a dickhead.'

'Ask for what you want, only take what you need, and be who you want to be … but just don't be a dickhead.'

'Live your life on your own terms, and create your own path … and just don't be a dickhead.'

Now, I wish I could say that I have always brought this simple, sincere reminder into my journey so far at exactly the right moment every time I've needed to hear it, but of course that is far from the truth. It's surprisingly sunk in, and has come in handy in a lot of situations, but I've still done so many dickhead-ish things in my life. I've definitely made some dickhead-ish choices. But I can say that, here at forty-eight years of age and as a mother of three children, I still try every day to live by it. It's arguably the best advice I have ever been given.

Just don't be a dickhead.

My childhood was very unique. The first decade of my life with my family was split between two different environments. For half of each year, we lived in a little beach shack in a small lobster-fishing village in the southeast of South Australia called Southend. With a population of only 198 people – a lot of them with the last name Chambers – it may have seemed small to some, but compared to my other life it was like a big city. We spent the other half of each year continuously travelling, living in a four-wheel-drive Toyota Land Cruiser and driving around the Nullarbor Plain and other remote areas in the Australian outback.

I was three weeks old when my parents first took me travelling into the outback. It was 1976. Aimlessly roaming mostly isolated places in South Australia and Western Australia while my dad hunted foxes and rabbits for a living. This was back when fox fur and rabbit

meat were lucrative trades in Australia. Certainly not a job that any of us would choose now of course, but these were different times, and Dad came from a long line of Chambers hunters and gatherers. My great-grandfather Stan Chambers had grown up in the Southend and Beachport area with a young Aboriginal boy called Lanky, who was from the South Australian Bungandidj tribe (which was known as the Boandik tribe when I was a kid) and would later go on to become a legendary tracker for local police, using his tracking ability and natural instincts to help solve crimes. Lanky taught my great-grandfather to hunt with a mix of survival skills and intuition he had learnt from his ancestors, and Grandpa Stan then passed these skills down through the Chambers generations. This became our normal.

The world was certainly a very different place back then. But our world was quite different again. When I look back on the memories of my childhood, my heart fills with joy and gratitude to be able to share such a unique upbringing through music and stories, but at the time I was living it, it was just my childhood. Nothing more. Nothing less. Nothing interesting. Nothing exceptional. I was just a simple little kid living by the sea and living in the outback. I had no idea that we were creating such a rare ordinary.

• • •

While our extended Chambers family held the small town of Southend together during the colder parts of the year, my immediate family chose the lifestyle of wandering gypsies, travelling to a different place most nights across one of the largest deserts in the world. The Nullarbor Plain is around 200,000 square kilometres between the Great Victoria Desert and the Great Australian Bight.

Almost every night on sundown, after Nash and I had taken turns having a bath in a plastic storage bin with rationed water heated on the campfire, we would pack up our camp, then head out hunting for the night.

My dad had made bunks in the back of the Land Cruiser for us all to sleep in, and we towed a small van that he had also made by hand, which stored all of our supplies and a tiny living area to provide shelter from the weather if needed. While my dad drove and hunted through the night, the rest of us would get into our bunks and go off to sleep. We travelled a lot of the time on rough dirt roads, or even off-road completely on uncharted territory, and I would usually fall straight asleep every night. Always with the sound of gunfire from high-powered hunting rifles echoing around me. Our normal. Needless to say I can sleep through pretty much anything these days.

But sometimes, late at night, after I knew my mum was asleep, I would sneak up and hang out with my dad. He would let me be in charge of the spotlight to find the foxes and the rabbits, and while we waited we listened to his favourite music on cassette tapes. He told me stories about the music he shared with his family when he was young, sitting around their kitchen table in the '50s, all singing old gospel songs together. He also told me about playing guitar in bands with his mates in the '60s, before I was born, and how he taught my mum to play the bass guitar in the '70s when they first met so they could make music together. He even told me how he went on TV playing music one time, which I thought meant my dad might have actually been famous in another life. A TV show … on actual TV!

'The show was called *New Faces*,' he said. 'The comedian and actor Paul Hogan was even on the same episode as me!'

'What does he do now, Dad?' I asked.

'Well, he's a big movie star in Hollywood.'

I looked at my dad and earnestly replied, 'You really showed him, didn't you, Dad?'

My dad was the coolest person I knew. He probably still is.

It's through my dad that I first found my connection with music.

• • •

In the still, dark, early hours of the morning, my dad would find some random place for us to camp. Usually hundreds of miles from where he'd left earlier on that evening, and a long, long way from any kind of civilisation. It was time to settle in for the night and get some sleep.

Every morning when we woke up, we were in a new place that we had never, ever seen before. Nash and I would always wake up first, excited to see what our home looked like that day. We'd gaze out the window of the Land Cruiser together, then turn to each other with a look that said, 'Yep, it looks exactly the same as yesterday – again.'

Through our hopefulness, we kinda always knew that everywhere out there pretty much looked the same. Saltbush. Flat horizon. Red dirt. But we didn't care. We had the biggest backyard in the whole world, and we were always ready to explore.

Mornings were the time to investigate every part of our new camp. To scope out potential cubbyhouses. We would find and collect sticks – some for firewood, some just to play with. We would play hide-and-seek in the saltbush. Nash would teach me target shooting with a slug gun or a bow and arrow. We would play make-believe games and gather rocks, giving them names and faces. We would try to catch wild animals … and sometimes successfully keep them as pets. We were always ready to use our imagination as much as we could. Plus, we often travelled and camped with another family – my

dad's cousin and his wife and three children – so we sometimes had other kids to play with too.

When my mum got up, it was time for home-schooling. She would drag out our lesson books and for an hour or two we'd learn our times tables and ABCs around the open campfire. My dad would sleep the latest, then spend a lot of the day working and preparing the fox skins. He would always have hunted some food for us to eat the night before, so my mum would start preparing the camp oven for the slow cook of the kangaroo tail soup or the wild rabbit stew.

Mum would get us kids to help keep the fire going throughout the day, and Dad would then get us to help get things ready for the night ahead. So, while most kids in the world were busy with chores like 'doing the dishes' and 'taking out the garbage', I thought it was quite normal to be 'lighting cooking fires' and 'reloading bullets to use to hunt our next meal'.

This was life in outback Australia for a kid in the '70s.

Create your own normal.

We had no real connection to the outside world at all while we were living out there. No phones, no radio signal.

I do remember, towards the end of our hunting seasons, my parents bringing a small TV and a Betamax video player out there with us. But being so far from any kind of TV station reception meant I had no other choice but to watch the one and only movie we had brought with us – *Lone Wolf McQuade* – every day for six months. And I did.

So, for the most part, there wasn't really any form of outside

entertainment available in our lives. (Aside from what Chuck Norris could continually bring to us.) But I would later discover that not having the distraction of mainstream entertainment was much more of a blessing than a curse, as it would leave room and space for the greatest inspirations of my life: imagination, creativity, music.

My dad would often bring out the acoustic guitar on a Friday night. (We didn't hunt on Friday nights for a while for religious reasons.) We would all sit around the campfire, and sing and play together as a family. Dad taught us old American country songs, Australian bush ballads, gospel hymns from his church days, old folk tunes and all the songs we knew from the tapes we listened to in the car. Johnny Cash, Hank Williams, Slim Dusty, Emmylou Harris, Larry Gatlin, Bobby Bare, Jackson Browne, Don Williams, Dolly Parton, the Carter family, The Amazing Rhythm Aces, Bob Dylan and even some Ray Charles.

This was my musical education.

My grounding in music.

My backbone.

My own conservatorium of music under the Southern Cross stars by the light of the campfire.

This is where my connection to music really began.

Music became a part of life. The outback life. The Chambers life.

Music is the backbone of my life.

'BACKBONE'

Don't poke a stick down a trapdoor spider hole.

2.

Listen to your inner foghorn

Deep down in the pit of my stomach, I believe wholeheartedly that I have an inner voice. A voice that guides me. I've always thought of her as my 'inner foghorn'. She can be a little screechy and a bit hard on the ears at times, like her sister voice, my singing foghorn, but they both always have heart and purpose behind them.

I am very proud of those two foghorns.

Don't get me wrong, I've had many times in my life when I've wished that my singing voice was completely different. She can definitely be a bit squawky and harsh at times too, and then on the flip side she sometimes feels weak and frail. My singing foghorn has many different sides. When I was younger, I would have moments where I hated that she sounded so fragile and shaky in one song, then in the next would be nasally and annoyingly loud. Over the years, I've seen lots of unfortunate people in my audience holding their hands over their ears as I hit the high notes or yodel through an old country song! But after a while I also started to see that there were some people in my audience who actually had their ears and their hearts open, who were being happily filled up by the sound of my voice.

I started to realise that this voice might have been given to me for a good reason. And that reason turned out to be: so that my heart can communicate with the world. And my heart has a lot to say. She has a lot to share.

When I got to know my singing voice a bit better, I realised I could use all these different dynamics in it – some I hadn't even discovered yet – to be able to express different kinds of songs, emotions and feelings that I could then write into melodies and lyrics. Sometimes, the emotion in my songs needed to feel soft and gentle to capture the essence of the purpose behind the song. Other times, the emotion needed to be powerful and strong to capture the essence of a different kind of purpose. And the truth was – and still is – I need to show all of these things, because I *am* all of these things. Sometimes I feel insecure, unsure, uncertain and afraid, and then sometimes I feel strong, powerful, sure of myself and confident.

So, eventually, instead of fighting my singing foghorn, I just started embracing her. I began feeling extremely grateful to have been given a voice that is able to reflect so many different things that I truly am and feel when I sing. Not everyone will like her. In fact many people will fucking hate her. And that's OK. For my purpose, my singing foghorn serves me and my heart very well.

My inner foghorn seems to work in a very similar way to my singing foghorn. Sometimes, she is quiet and subtle – like a light tapping on my chest or a whisper from my heart. That's when I call her my *little* inner foghorn. Other times, she is loud and assertive and hard to ignore – even when I try to. That's when I call her my *screechy* inner foghorn – and fuck, she is powerful. Commanding. A force to be reckoned with.

My inner foghorn represents all the different sides of me. But only the true sides of me. The real me. And she always shows up when I need her most – but I only really hear her when I turn down the outer noise. So, she might be there as my little inner foghorn, whispering quietly to me, and I ignore her – but, if I do that for too long, she eventually morphs into my screechy inner foghorn and screams at me like a death metal frontman.

Now, I know what you're probably thinking: 'Kase, you might wanna get checked out by a professional if you're hearing voices in your head?' But my inner foghorn's not an audible voice. There are no words, messages, demands or orders for me to follow out. She's more like a feeling deep inside me. An intuition. A compass for my heart and soul. She gives me subtle (or not-so-subtle) signs to let me know I'm on the right path. Or not.

I believe that everyone's path is their own. One of a kind. An authentic road for each of us. What is right for you may not be right for me. What is true for you may not be true for me. And there's a lot of noise out there telling us all how we are supposed to live our lives. What we should believe. How we should see things. What we should think and feel. But, in my eyes, every heart has its own journey to make. My inner foghorn is my guide for that journey.

She is the voice of my genuine heart.

The voice of my creative soul.

The voice of my no-bullshit gut.

The voice of my backbone.

She is filled with so much more wisdom than the rest of me. She's a fucking gem.

She leads with love and authenticity. She knows my path is supposed to be unique and soul-filling. She is open-minded, unconditioned and free-spirited.

She is humble, and doesn't need credit for her efforts.

She is giving and creative.

She's inspiring, brave and purposeful.

She's motivated and doesn't play games.

She won't waste time worrying about what other people think of her, and doesn't judge anyone else for having a different path.

She's kind and compassionate, but she doesn't take any shit from anyone either. She stands up for herself. She knows who she is. She knows who I am, deep down.

And I know who I am when I am tuned into her.

• • •

Unfortunately, the truth is, I don't always choose to tune into my inner foghorn. I don't always choose to listen to her. There are a lot of times in my life when I haven't heard her at all. In fact, sometimes I have even purposefully tuned her *out* and pretended she doesn't exist so that I can make stupid decisions.

There have been times when she's screamed at me and given me shitloads of obvious signs about where to go and what to choose and I have *still* ignored her. Instead, I've chosen to listen to my dickhead foghorn. Yep, there's another one. Another voice.

This one's a total dickhead, and she can be just as loud as my inner foghorn.

She throws around shiny things that appeal to my ego, and she distracts me from anything real or deep.

She only ever wants the quick fix, the easy way out and shallow gratification.

She's selfish, and doesn't really want to waste time doing any real work.

She's full of egotistical needs, and she makes fucking dumb decisions.

And, more often than not, she goes out of her way to give me lots of self-doubt and insecurities.

So, my whole life – then, now and ahead – all really boils down to the battle between my dickhead foghorn and my wise inner foghorn. It's all a matter of which one I'm going to choose to listen to.

Listen to your inner foghorn.

During the six months of each year that we spent hunting in the outback, our main way to get food supplies was to stop in at the small railway sidings – tiny little towns of only a few houses that sat along the railway lines that ran across the Nullarbor. These isolated places were where the railway workers and their families lived. They were supplied by the 'tea and sugar train', which was kinda like a moving grocery store that travelled through weekly. It'd stop, and the locals would be able to stock up with what they needed to get by.

We would time our visits into these towns, like Denman, Deakin and Forrest, so we could do our shopping on the train when it came through. Mum and I would get onto the carriage of the train with a little shopping basket, while Dad and Nash went to top up the tanks with town water and extra fuel. There wasn't a lot of choice on board. Mostly necessities, staples. The bread was often mouldy by the time we shopped, but we always still bought it, and just picked off the mouldy bits and ate it anyway.

We only needed enough supplies to get us through to the next stop, usually a few weeks away, but Mum would always get some cans of soft drink for us to enjoy together as a family. Coke, Fanta, lemonade and non-alcoholic Stoney ginger beer. A rare little indulgence. On special nights after dinner, the four of us would share one small can. It was always such a treat.

We took turns choosing the soft drink we'd have on those special occasions. My favourite was Fanta, then the lemonade, and then Coke, but ginger beer? Yuck! I couldn't stomach it, and wouldn't even drink it when someone else chose it. But ginger beer was my brother's favourite. Oh, he loved it more than any of them. It was always his first choice.

This one night when I was about seven and Nash was ten, we were all having dinner as a family, crammed up in the little van that Dad had made. Mum had cooked on the campfire outside, but when it was cold and windy we'd all get inside the van and gather round the small table to eat.

During the day, Nash had been particularly uncooperative with my mum and had got in trouble for it. His punishment was that, after dinner, he was to get NONE of the can of soft drink. It would be shared by only Mum, Dad and me.

After dinner, Mum said to me, 'What drink do you choose, Kase? You'll get a bit more than usual tonight because of your brother's behaviour. He misses out this time.'

I looked at Nash with an expression of extreme sisterly love and, just as if butter wouldn't melt in my mouth, I said, 'I choose ginger beer.' And I forced every disgusting mouthful down my throat, facing my envious brother the whole time. Then I put the can right there in front of him, and I smiled.

I had started being a dickhead already.

We are all capable of being a dickhead.

Our family would often camp quite close to the railway line that crosses from one side of Australia to the other. It's the longest straight railway line in the world, stretching 478 kilometres without a bend.

If my brother and I woke up in the morning and saw the railway line nearby, or even in the distance, there was a small bit of extra excitement that arose in us. That meant we already had a plan for the day ahead.

First, though, we had to fulfil our firewood-gathering duties, light the campfire, toast up our partially mouldy bread on the burnt-down coals for breakfast, then quickly get through the vaguely scheduled part of the day where our conventional education was considered mildly important. After home-schooling in our big open classroom was done, it was free time. Hooray!

Nash and I didn't need to tell each other the plan too much. We already knew what we had to get sorted. We'd head over to our cousins' camp – usually a few hundred metres away in a similar set-

up to ours – and see if they'd finished school too. Then with cousins Narelle, Traci and Clint ready and eager, it was time to raid our parents' clothes in the homemade cupboards in the four-wheel drives. Once we had our costumes, it was straight into rehearsals.

We would all choose our acting parts for the performance. Narelle, Traci, Nash and I would pull rank, and give the smallest part to Clint, because he was the youngest. Then it was time to write and learn all of our lines. We would usually pick some old, well-known story or nursery rhyme, then put our own spin on it. So 'The Hare and the Tortoise' became, in our Nullarbor version, 'The Rabbit and the Wombat'.

Having practised over and over, with some to-be-expected arguing over the lines, it was finally done. Show time. We'd gather up the only four people within a 300-kilometre radius of our camp (our parents), collect their 20-cent entry fee to the widely critically

acclaimed concert ahead, and get ready to give the performance of a lifetime! And that it was – for me, anyway. I would get so swept up in every magical scene of the whole production. My heart and soul would openly deliver every line, and my overly dramatic movements and expressions would take over my whole body like an exaggerated over-actor on Broadway. It was as though each scene was the most important moment that had ever existed in my world.

I was already a performer. I loved it. I felt so alive and vibrant being out on that stage. OK, there was no actual stage. But I didn't care. In my eyes, there was. My red-dirt stage may not have even been raised off the ground, but my little inner foghorn was already telling me that this was my home. Something within me unlocked every time I opened up my creative performer heart. I didn't care that the audience was only four people. I may not have even noticed if they'd all got up and left. My performing spirit had been set free.

• • •

At the end, we would all bow, and the 'crowd' would give a standing ovation and go wild. Of course, our parents didn't have any other entertainment to choose from, so they were a fairly easy audience to win over, but I still treated it like it had been the performance of a lifetime to a crowd of thousands.

Then, our parents would throw a few extra coins into the makeshift donation box that we had left out accidentally on purpose during the performance. We'd gather up the money, and share it all between us – Clint getting a little less than everyone else, because he was the youngest. Of course.

With all of us living hundreds of miles away from any kind of shop or store, in such an isolated area, using this money to buy anything was obviously never really our incentive. It wasn't even on our radar. We had better plans for our coins.

We would sit and wait. And listen.

The Nullarbor has an incredible sound. Silence, with the occasional lone crow or wild dingo. Sometimes a train. There it was! In the distance. A low, faint rumble. No mistaking that sound. The moment we heard it, us five kids would grab our coins and run as fast as we could all the way down to the railway line. We knew full well that we still had plenty of time before the train got anywhere near us, but also that it could be days before another came along so there was to be no chance of us missing it.

We would then place all our coins carefully on the tracks, trying to find some kind of marker close by – an odd-shaped stick or a railway bolt, something so we knew where to come back to and look for our coins afterwards.

Then it was time to make our way back to camp for some more

waiting. It was always a slower trek back to our camp, all of us holding the hope that the train would be closer than we thought. Waiting. Waiting. And more waiting. It was always *further* than we thought. Always further than it sounded. A train out there could be heard from at least 20 kilometres away, and sometimes took half an hour to finally get to us.

But the wait was always worth it.

Eventually, the train would reach the carefully watched spot where we had planted our coins, then pass on by towards its destination. Never without the train driver first giving us a toot on the way past – people out this far were a rare sight for him as well. Sometimes, he would even throw a newspaper out the window for us. It might have been a week or two old by then, but time didn't mean much to us. While our parents would give the driver a casual wave, us five kids would be cheering and jumping up and down, screaming like a celebrity had come to town and given us a brief acknowledgement from afar just to make our day.

Then it was time to collect. We would run as fast as our little legs could take us back down to the railway line and begin our search for the flattened coins. Little Clint was always trailing behind, of course, but just as eager to find his precious treasure. As the train ran over the coins, they'd often get flicked up from the back of the wheels and into the dirt or stones running along the side of the tracks. This was how we'd learnt, after our first few attempts at this, how important those markers were when it came to finding our finished products.

'Hooray! Hooray! I found one! I found one!'

It was a welcome result if we found one coin out of the two or three we'd each placed, as sometimes they flicked so far from the tracks there was no chance of ever finding them. Sometimes, luck would be

on our side and a coin would stay on the track. The discovery was like what I imagine a Lotto win to feel like. If one of us found more than one coin, we'd hand it over to a cousin or a sibling who hadn't been so lucky that day, so that everyone always got something.

I would look down at my flattened coin in my little palm, and it was like I had just been handed a million dollars. My eyes wide with the discovery of the new life it had taken on – something that I could never have foreseen in the coin's original shape. The print had mostly disappeared, and it was smooth when I ran my fingers across it. My heart was full with the joy at having taken something so standard and turned it into this special, one-of-a-kind creation.

I didn't know it, but I was already choosing my value in money. A value that I would carry through my life. It was not about profit. It was not about greed. It was not about conventional currency. It was all about intention. Earning money doing something I loved, then turning that money into something meaningful to me.

I am thankful for my first-ever job, and my first-ever co-worker, the Nullarbor Train.

Money only has the value that I choose to put on it.

Don't save your beautiful things for a special occasion. There is no moment more special than right now.

3.

Trust in your higher old mate

Over the warmer months of every year, we spent a lot of the time living in a little three-bedroom beach shack in Southend that my parents had bought in the early '70s. From there, my brother and I would catch the bus to the nearby town of Rendelsham to attend a 'normal' school. There were only about 30 kids in the whole school, but it still felt pretty crowded to us.

My mum had grown up about four hours north, on a poultry farm just outside of Mannum in South Australia with her mum, her stepdad and one older sister. Southend was Dad's hometown and, as the oldest of seven siblings in a big religious family, he'd carried his Seventh-day Adventist beliefs with him well into his adulthood. Kinda. A lot of his Christian faith had been well ingrained in him from a young age, and in my early years he and Mum were mostly abiding by the Adventist convention while living in Southend. Attending church regularly. Honouring the day of rest from Friday sundown to Saturday sundown by not working, not watching television and not going out during that time. They didn't drink alcohol or eat pork or shellfish, and ate only some red meat. I remember my dad saying he found it extra hard when he was a little kid not to eat shellfish, because his dad was a lobster fisherman. I certainly don't think I would have been able to dig deep enough to find that kind of willpower.

Clearly my brother did not share Dad's childhood obedience. Whenever Nash was given lolly money to walk down to the local shop and get us both a treat, he would instead spend it all on slices of luncheon meat called fritz, which contained pork, which we were obviously not allowed to have. He would eat it all by the time he got home, so Mum and Dad wouldn't find out. No lollies for me. A little fair payback for the can of ginger beer, maybe?

But, even underneath my parents' faithful devotion, there was uncertainty. They began to feel like being under a strict religious regime and being discouraged from ever questioning the ways of the church was not quite matching up with who they were anymore. Something just didn't feel right to them.

When we were in the outback the rest of the year, the freedom we all felt was undeniable. It had already given my parents a little more of the 'when in Rome' approach – not having a whole lot of food choice out there meant that kangaroo and rabbit were allowed back on the menu. Eventually, their many unanswered questions – and the disruption it caused even asking – didn't quite resonate with their inner foghorns, and my parents turned in their letter of resignation to the church. They still kept a lot of the values, principles and faith they had learnt over the years, but decided to match up their belief system with their preferred lifestyle – instead of the other way around.

I'm still not a hundred per cent sure what the deal breaker was that occurred, but I know the story of my dad being extremely unhappy about not being able to watch a Merle Haggard TV special because it aired on a Friday night, so that would probably have to be a fairly sure bet.

• • •

My parents have never told me what to believe. They've never even told me what I should believe. But I think they showed me *how* to believe.

They showed me how to believe in myself.

They showed me that belief comes from within. That belief doesn't have to be about what someone tells you it has to be, but more about what resonates with your inner truth. Everyone's belief can be different.

And they also showed me that my belief is always mine to decide. That it's OK to pick my own beliefs, and then change them if they don't match up with me anymore.

They also gave me the opportunity to open my mind to the possibility of something bigger than myself.

Something greater.

Something higher.

Something to believe in.

It's OK to change my mind.

'SOMETHING TO BELIEVE IN'

I've chosen my beliefs in my life. I've changed my beliefs in my life. I've taken out new beliefs. I've gone back to old beliefs. I've modified them to match up with my always-changing self.

I don't really mind what a person or book tells me I should or shouldn't believe, or how I should do it, but for most of my life I've felt pretty sure that I am sharing this journey with something bigger. Something higher than myself. Something higher than all of us.

Now, I'm not exactly sure what that is.

Some like to call it God. Some like to call it the universe. Some like to call it Buddha or Allah or Jesus. Some find it in Mother Nature, or within themselves. Some don't believe in anything at all.

I guess I believe that all of these things can all be true. All of these things can all be real. For any of us.

Whatever we call our higher power or, even if we don't have one, whatever belief we choose to share this journey with – if it helps us to live our best lives, not purposely hurt others, if it helps us to honour our true selves and get through hard times, if it encourages us to tune into our inner foghorns and supports our authentic paths, then it all sounds pretty fucking good to me.

Call me a believer!

Belief comes from within.

I am forever changing, so I am forever checking in with myself and my beliefs and opinions to make sure they do still match up with who I am deep down.

I believe it takes true faith in myself to let beliefs go that don't resonate with who I am anymore, and true courage in myself to open my mind enough to new beliefs that might help me to grow even more. I choose not to be locked into anything.

So I guess right now I have kind of a hybrid faith in something bigger. Something I can trust in when I need. A higher guide to follow. Like an old, dependable friend who always has my back no matter what. I try to trust in this friend even when things get a little off track. Especially when things get a little off track. I call this friend my higher old mate, and I think she has a bigger plan. One that I can't always see.

I don't believe I work for my higher old mate, and I don't believe she works for me either. We work together in this unique journey. Sometimes I need to follow her to where I need be, and sometimes I need to lead the way myself. I don't sit back and wait for her to do shit for me, but sometimes I do need her help.

Sometimes I'll be guided by her blindly, and sometimes I can see every little bit of her magic.

Sometimes I need to take control – just dig in to get shit done while she sits back – and then sometimes I need to close my eyes and trust in her and surrender.

Sometimes I need to have enough faith in her that everything happens for a reason even if I can't see it, but sometimes it's up to me to decide what that reason is gonna be.

Sometimes she shows me obvious signs that I see clearly, and sometimes they are subtle and hidden in *Seinfeld* episodes.

Sometimes I shout at her from the rooftops, and sometimes she tells me to just sit down and shut the fuck up.

But over the years I've realised that, when I believe in something bigger than myself, I feel bigger *within* myself. My heart feels bigger.

My soul feels bigger. My love feels bigger. My trust feels bigger. My creativity feels bigger.

There are some days when I feel so capable and confident, and I just quietly lean over to my higher old mate and I whisper, 'I've got this.'

Then some days I feel weak and lost and I question whether my higher old mate even exists anymore. These are usually the days when she leans over to me and says, 'Don't worry, Kase. I've got this one.'

Trust in your higher old mate.

Living a big chunk of my childhood in such an isolated, secluded and open environment was extremely liberating and freeing for us kids. And for my parents, I'm sure. Our surroundings on the Nullarbor Plain, like our parents, were always so encouraging of us kids just being free spirits.

When my brother and I were in the outback, we were never restricted by conventional or societal expectations in the way a lot of other kids growing up in more populated areas at the time were – and certainly nothing even close to the extent of most kids growing up today.

Our parents did put a few rules in place though.

- Don't waste water.
- Don't touch the rifles under any circumstances.
- If you're out exploring and you hear the car horn honk three times, come back to camp.
- Take your shoes off when you climb into the bunks in the

Land Cruiser, because if Dad finds a bindi-eye prickle or a three-corner jack in his bed he will lose his shit.

- Only use green wood to carve out your toasting fork, or it will burn on the fire when you use it.

So I guess they were rigid about some things. But, for the most part, my outback childhood was filled with a lot of freedom. My brother and I always felt free to explore and investigate. To ask questions and gather information. To learn how to do new things, and try stuff out on our own. To use our imaginations and think for ourselves. To develop opinions and beliefs, and change them whenever we wanted. To laugh and cry, and never worry about what we looked like to anyone else. To get our clothes and our hands dirty doing fun things that had no other gain besides just passing the time. To tell stories and create songs and make believe. To scream and sing as loud as we could every day. To say whatever we felt whenever we wanted.

• • •

The fox-skin buyers would come out to our camp every few months to meet us and buy up, and sometimes they would bring other people with them. One time, I remember they landed in a helicopter, and the pilot even let all us kids sit in it for a bit.

Another time, one of the regular buyers brought his eighteen-year-old son, Dean, out to help him. Dean had the cutest little puppy I had ever seen. Our faithful, grubby, shaggy, unclipped family hunting dog, who was called Liquorice and was technically supposed to be a French poodle, travelled around the outback with us every year. I loved 'Licky' dearly, but it's hard to compete with a newly born puppy for an eight-year-old girl's attention.

'What's his name?' I asked Dean.

Obviously, Dean wasn't that restricted by societal conventions either – and he didn't care much about appropriate language – because he just said, 'I just call him a little cunt.'

In my innocent, trusting mind I gathered that must have been the puppy's name, so I spent the rest of the afternoon happily calling out, 'Little cunt! Little cunt! Come here, little cunt!'

A free spirit can't truly fly with conventional rules.

Just because I don't believe in it doesn't mean it's not true for someone else.

4.

Everything is a stepping stone

I guess my childhood was sheltered in a lot of ways, but it was also mostly unaffected by judgement, discrimination and conservative rules. I never remember a time when my parents told us kids to 'be on our best behaviour' in front of certain people, or to pretend we were something that we were not. We were always just encouraged to be ourselves. Our true selves.

But life wouldn't stay like that forever.

Eventually our worlds expanded. Beyond the Nullarbor, beyond the outback, beyond the small beach town of Southend and the local school. Beyond freedom. To what some might call the 'real world'. Society. High school.

Things started looking very different for me. I went from my classroom around the campfire with mostly one classmate to a regular-sized high school in Millicent, South Australia, with over 300 teenagers. Fuck.

I struggled. To fit in. To adapt. To go from the free-spirited, simple little lifestyle I was used to – the one created by my parents, my first influencers – to the firm structure of a mainstream system. High school, to me, felt riddled with conformity, conditioning, uniformity, authority, conventionality and all these fucking rules.

Most of the time I just felt lost and out of place in this new world. I didn't resonate at all with any of it. Not the hierarchy or the student pecking order. Not the competitiveness of sport or the rivalry in music. Not the desperation to be part of the school clique or the popularity contests. Not the teasing and talking behind people's backs. It was all just weird and foreign to me. I knew the kids in all the different groups, but I didn't really feel a part of any of them. I just didn't feel like I really belonged there at all.

That first year of high school felt like the longest of my life.

Then, one day, through my self-conscious confusion, these expressive words came up from deep inside me. Lots of words, sentences and phrases, all creeping up to the surface and wanting me to let them out. Firstly, in the form of creative stories, then turning into what I would eventually call 'becoming a songwriter'. Maybe this new creative side I was beginning to really discover was actually a gift from long ago from my higher old mate?

It was like the saviour that I never knew I needed.

This place from which I would write lyrics, create stories and sing felt safe and open. I felt naturally connected to it. A connection that felt different from any I'd had before.

This little creative house that I was building inside myself was starting to feel like a home. A home that was free and uninhibited, without rules or judgement. No boundaries or barriers. It felt more like my childhood. But, unlike the outback, this creative home wasn't hundreds of miles away – it was right here. It was always right here. Inside me. I carried this home with me wherever I went, all the time, and I could visit it whenever I wanted. I could turn to it and set myself free in it whenever I needed. It was a place where I could just be me – the real me. A place where I felt calm and grounded. Where I didn't care whether I was different. In fact, I loved being different when I was in my creative home.

This was my other 'new' world.

And, in what would maybe end up being the most beautiful part of all, I eventually discovered that these two 'new' worlds that I was living in – my creative home and the 'real world' – were actually not so far apart after all. Over the next few years, I started to realise that I could bring parts of my beautiful creative home with me into the 'real world'. Instead of seeing these two places as worlds apart, I could use this creativity to connect them. To bring them together. And to connect to other people, too. Sharing my thoughts, my words, my feelings and my voice didn't separate us into different worlds – it actually drew us all closer.

I started to see the 'real world' through a different lens – through the eyes of my free creative spirit – and everything looked prettier. More beautiful. More appealing to my heart. And I started to see the creativity and free spirit in other people as well. I started making actual friends with lots of kids from all of the different groups – the popular kids, the outcasts, the academics, the sporties, the misunderstood – and I found connections with all of them, because I had found a connection with myself.

I began seeing the worth in everyone and everything else, because

I had seen the worth in myself.

I still didn't belong to any one group, but I didn't really need to. I was just learning to be me.

As I write this now, I'm also starting to see how my struggle and learning curve to fit in at high school repeated itself again later on in my life, in the struggle and learning curve I felt while trying to fit into the music industry, where I often felt out of place. Both environments seemed weird and foreign to me at times, and I wanted to close up and run away. But, in both, once I started just connecting back to myself through my free spirit and my creativity – and once I stopped trying to keep up with anyone else and tuned into my inner foghorn – I started to see the beauty all around me. I was able to stay outside of any of the groups and cliques, and just create my own home. A place where I could feel more like me.

Then, I could draw the beautiful things I wanted from all the different worlds, link them together in harmony, and let go of the battle between. I ended up feeling a part of something without having to abandon myself to get it. But, unlike this teenage self-discovery I was going through, the music industry self-discovery as an adult would take me a little bit longer, cut a little bit deeper and not quite stick the first time. Or the second. Or the third.

I guess the further away I got from my childhood, the harder it became to live in the outer world with my inner free spirit.

(Ironically I actually failed music in high school, according to the education department, but if there had been a grading in 'music connection' I like to think I would've gotten an A+!)

When I grow up I wanna be a kid again.

I don't really remember feeling too much actual fear during my early childhood. Of course, there was always the chance of a large army of meat ants crawling up my legs if I was playing in their nest. Or the threat of a western taipan or eastern brown snake sliding down from the firewood stored on the roof of the Land Cruiser and through the hole in the roof into the vehicle while we slept. Or the danger of driving into a giant chasm in the ground big enough to swallow a car (actually more possible on the Nullarbor Plain than you'd think). But I was usually sound asleep whenever Dad saw any of those things, so I really didn't carry many of these types of fears with me into adulthood.

Dangerous wild animals still don't faze me much now, and I don't stay up at night (very often) worrying about a giant chasm in the road when I drive out my driveway. But, for a while after joining the 'real world', I started becoming afraid of something that's much less life-threatening but can be equally as damaging. A much more common fear.

Yep, I was developing a fear of criticism.

I was nine years old when I made my first actual on-stage singing appearance – a real gig in front of people who weren't just my parents. It was around this time that my family began to spend a lot more time in Southend and less in the outback, as my brother and I had our high-school years coming up, so the gig was at our local club in Southend. My best friend, Caddie, and I performed two songs popular on the radio at the time – Cyndi Lauper's 'Time After Time' and Dire Straits' 'Walk of Life' – with my parents as part of the country band they'd just started.

I say we 'performed', but actually Caddie and I both just stood there like deer caught in the headlights, barely able to move, so I'm

not sure there was much actual 'performance' going on. But we must have enjoyed it on some level deep down, because we did it again. Over the coming months, we learnt a few more songs and performed them at more gigs with Mum and Dad. We felt like we were kinda getting used to it after a while, but in reality the two of us were still just standing there, not saying a word, singing blankly like startled little deer every time.

Throughout my teenage years, I went on to sing and play many local gigs with the family band, and I slowly got more used to actually performing instead of just standing there. I will never forget one gig in particular. It was at a local pony club, and I was covering Kim Wilde's version of 'You Keep Me Hangin' On'. (I thought it was her song at the time, because she was always on the radio singing it. I had never even heard of The Supremes.) Then, when I was halfway through the song, I forgot the lyrics. I went completely blank.

What is the second verse? I thought. *What is the next word? Where am I in the song? What song am I singing? What is my own name?!*

I clearly remember the room being full of hundreds of attentive people, and every single eye in the place was directed straight at me, frozen in fear in front of them. Now, realistically, I may have embellished that memory a little over the years, given that I don't think we ever played to hundreds of people at any of those gigs – and they were certainly never attentive! It's much more likely that, actually, barely anyone in the room was even looking at me, let alone noticed that I'd forgotten the lyrics. But I crumbled. Fear had taken over.

I looked over at my dad, and he said casually, 'Don't worry. Just sing the first verse again.'

But my little stomach was all churned up, and it felt like the floor was trying to swallow me whole like something from a Tom and Jerry cartoon. And I kinda wanted it to. I just wanted to disappear.

I burst into tears, and ran off the stage mid-song. (Again, I actually don't even think there was a stage – I'm pretty sure we just played our set behind two big beams in the corner of the room between the kitchen and the stables.)

Outside, I sat by myself and I cried.

When the set was finished, my mum came out and put her arm round me. 'Everything's gonna be alright,' she said.

But I firmly declared to her that I would never, ever go back on stage or sing ever again for the rest of my life. And I meant it. That feeling of fear was excruciating.

We sat there together for a bit, and I'm sure Mum was trying to be supportive, but I was obviously the only person in the entire world who had ever felt anything like this, so my life as I knew it was probably over.

When Mum went back inside to join Dad for the last set, I sneakily watched from outside. And I started to notice that, as the night wore on, the music got a little bit louder and the crowd got a little bit happier. People began to cheer and applaud, and they even started dancing. Everyone was having such a good time.

Mmmmmm … this is interesting.

So, even though I was dying inside, experiencing the worst moment of my life to date, the world hadn't actually stopped spinning? Interesting indeed.

In fact, not only did the world not stop spinning, but people were even able to have some fun.

Will I ever be able to have fun again? I wondered. Then: *It certainly does look like my kinda fun happening in there …*

And, as my fear of missing out started to over-ride my fear of criticism, I sheepishly wandered back inside. Then, pretending nothing had happened, I got back up on the 'stage' and pushed through and sang three more songs.

I didn't die, and I even remembered all the lyrics.

Fear can be a dickhead.

This marked the start of The Dead Ringer Band, created by my parents in the '80s. My brother and I eventually joined it permanently, and all of us would open it up to many of our friends and fellow musicians along the way over the next twelve years. Held together with Mum on bass guitar, Dad on lead guitar, banjo, mandolin, dobro, slide guitar and vocals, Nash swapping between drums, guitar and vocals, and

me mostly just singing – but eventually also playing rhythm guitar after seeing Melissa Etheridge in concert.

We started out booking mostly local gigs in southeast Australia, but it wasn't long before the love of performing wormed its way into all our hearts and we took our band out on the road. We would travel to pubs, clubs and town halls in small regional places where Mum had booked in low-paying gigs or sometimes private parties. We played small country music festivals and Camel Cup races in outback towns and Aboriginal communities with other local bands.

At our gigs, we'd play all of our favourite covers from artists like the Eagles, Emmylou Harris, Creedence Clearwater Revival, Johnny Cash, J. J. Cale, Merle Haggard, Slim Dusty, George Jones, Dolly Parton and Gram Parsons. Also, I would attempt (badly) to cover mainstream pop hits by the likes of The Bangles, Roxette and Tiffany. I'm not sure our audience really understood at that point what kind of band we were stylistically (or that we did!), given we would jump

from 'I'm So Lonesome I Could Cry' to 'Walk Like an Egyptian'. But that didn't matter. We were loving every minute of it.

At some of the gigs, the pubs would give us a few free soft drinks, a counter meal and a room to stay in for the night. But the rest of the time, we each had a swag, the family four-wheel drive and the old Nullarbor van (which Dad had converted into a good place to carry all our musical instruments and our PA system, with a makeshift kitchen on the side). We would light a campfire just outside of the town we were playing in, set up our camp, cook our meals, then head back into town to play the gig. Then, after the gig was finished, we'd pack up all our instruments and our PA gear, and head back to our campsite and sleep in our swags under the stars. (Rainy nights sucked a bit.) The next morning, we'd leave to find a truck-stop roadhouse for showers, then drive hundreds of kilometres to the next town and the next gig.

I was loving the lifestyle and quite at home on stage by this point, but my dad still had to introduce all of my songs for me because I had developed a fear of talking over the microphone. It was unusual because I really wouldn't shut up off stage! Talking was my favourite pastime. Still is. If you happen to have seen me in concert any time within the last thirty years, I'm sure you'll find this silent phase a tad hard to believe, given that I generally talk waaaaay too much on stage and have a bad habit of over-sharing when I'm on the microphone. But, back then, my fear of talking on stage was real. I would sing my little heart out over that microphone, song after song, but saying a word without a melody attached? That seemed absolutely impossible.

Then, one night in my late teens, after many failed attempts to push through my fear, my little inner foghorn decided she had too much to say. She wasn't going to hold back any longer. And, as I stood on stage in front of that microphone during the silence between songs, I mustered up my courage, dug just a little bit deeper, opened my mouth and – not knowing if churned-up vomit would come shooting out – I said:

'This is a Nicolette Larson song.'

And then I started singing 'That's More About Love (Than I Wanted to Know)'.

Not wanting to make a big deal about the little breakthrough they had just witnessed, my mum, dad and Nash all tried to not look over at me. With their constant encouragement and support (and a last push from my inner foghorn), I'd finally faced my fear. I'd talked over that microphone. But I'm sure, in hindsight, somewhere deep down, my family are probably wishing they never let that beast out of its cage.

Fear is sometimes just a fucking killjoy.

In 1991, my dad heard that one of his biggest Australian musical inspirations ever, the legendary Slim Dusty, was looking for song ideas. Dad's cousin Kevvy Chambers had heard Slim talking on the radio about the devastating drought that had affected outback farmers at the time, and he'd said he was wanting to record a song that reflected what was happening.

Dad had written a few songs before, but mostly he just played guitar and sang. He'd never met his idol, Slim, and didn't really know anything at all about the music industry, but he decided he would just sit down with a pen and paper, a guitar and his heart on his sleeve, and write that song. There was probably a very *slim* chance (see what I did there?) of his song ever actually reaching the legend himself, but Dad put it down on a cassette tape anyway and sent it off in the mail to Slim Dusty's producer in Sydney.

A few months passed, and the song fell from Dad's mind.

Then, one day, he got a phone call from a stranger. This guy was claiming to be Slim Dusty.

Mmmmm, sounds a bit suss, thought Dad. *Probably one of my mates pulling my leg.*

So he laughed down the line, and accused the man on the phone of not being a very good prankster. Then he was just about to hang up when the stranger said, 'Your song "Things Are Not the Same on the Land" is exactly what I'm looking for. I'd like to record it.'

It was real. Dad was really talking to one of his biggest musical heroes on the planet. The man who had inspired him to take his whole family out on the road, touring music, just like Slim and his wife had done with their family in the early years. Dad was overjoyed.

It's always worth a shot.

We had never heard of a Golden Guitar, but the following year – thanks to Slim's version of it – that song was nominated for and then won Song of the Year at the Golden Guitar Awards at the Tamworth Country Music Festival. (It was the furthest thing from my mind, of course, that one day I would actually be lucky enough to win twenty-four Golden Guitars!) So, we decided to take our family band up to the country music capital of Australia for the first time. We figured we'd try out this 'making it big in music' thing that everyone seemed to be talking about.

It was time to splurge a bit. To go in style. We upgraded the swags to a four-man tent, oblivious to the fact it's often over 40 degrees Celsius during that time of year in Tamworth. Then we rolled into Australia's beloved home of country music unannounced and unprepared during festival time, ready to get a gig. We had no idea that these gigs were exclusively booked years in advance, and we got a firm 'no' from every pub, club, hall, stage, agent and promoter in town. So we figured we'd just busk in the street.

We set up right in front of the Central Hotel on Peel Street in the town centre (this was back in the days before you needed a busking permit). As well as our family, our band included a few of our fellow South Australian musicians: Beccy Sturtzel (who would later become Beccy Cole), and Trev Warner on the fiddle and banjo with his son Kym Warner on the mandolin. We busked every night of the music festival, and built up more of a crowd with every gig.

And we must have impressed the promoter of the Gympie Music Muster as they wandered by, because we were booked to play on a small stage there the following year. That festival performance then turned into more appearances at the Music Muster over the next few years. When a representative from EMI Records called Leon Concannon just so happened to be walking past our stage when we started playing one of those gigs, it eventually led to my first major-label record deal, which would then go on to launch my entire solo career.

Everything is a stepping stone.

The song 'Things Are Not the Same on the Land' marked the beginning of a beautiful relationship between our family and Slim Dusty and his wife, Joy McKean. From then on, they supported, nurtured and championed our journey into the country music industry.

On the one hand there was a lot about those early years in the industry that was confusing and discouraging for us. We got a lot of 'no's, were relentlessly told by industry heavyweights that our 'look' wasn't country enough, repeatedly heard from venue owners that we didn't play the right songs, were informed over and over by radio stations that we didn't 'sound' the way that a country band should sound, and got disqualified from talent quests for not wearing cowboy boots or not introducing our songs the right way. One person even told us, 'I'll make sure you never work in this industry again.' But having Slim and Joy flying our flag in their unique, renegade-leadership way helped to give us motivation and a belief in ourselves that over-rode all of it.

I learnt from the best of the best that going out of your way to support, encourage and show belief in other people who are following their dreams can make more of a difference than you can ever know.

No matter how big or small, how solid or shaky, how stable or unsteady the ground underfoot, every little stone that I have ever stepped on has always led to another ... (Except when I had kidney stones. That just fucking hurt.)

After that first visit to Tamworth, we started to return every year and The Dead Ringer Band finally began getting a few local gigs around town.

This one night, we got the gig time-slot in the front bar of the West Tamworth League Club, and we were playing outside the main auditorium while people waited in line for the main show, which was ticketed, to open its doors. No one was really listening or applauding. Punters would line up on the other side of the room, barely noticing us, just waiting for their turn to enter the ticketed show and see their favourite country star. The bar was busy, the pokies in the next room were noisy, and the cooks would scream out meal numbers from the bistro whenever food was ready to be picked up. But I didn't care. I was a teenager getting out of school. I had a cool job. I was singing my favourite songs, on a stage with every bit of my heart bursting out of me. My soul was on fire, and I was in my own little world. My own little musical world, where I always knew who I was.

Then the time came for a break, so I wandered over to the side door, as there was no backstage or green room. A cool, edgy, good-looking guy walked up to me with an unusually beautiful mix of extreme confidence and genuine warmth, and he said to me, 'Nice gig. You sing like you don't give a shit what anyone thinks of you. I like that.'

I knew who this guy was. And if not giving a shit what people thought was good enough for Keith Urban, then it was good enough for me.

Keith wasn't world famous yet, but he kinda was in my eyes. I had seen him play at a local pub, the Avoca Beach Hotel, on the central coast of New South Wales. (An area we'd later relocate our entire family to partly because Keith Urban played there regularly. Not even kidding.) And, when I'd watched him play, I couldn't believe how someone could make only a few people in a little bar feel like they were in a massive stadium watching the biggest entertainer of all time. I was in awe, every time.

I'd also met him once before in person, although he wouldn't have remembered it. It was in the little town of Ararat in Victoria, and we had crossed paths on tour. He'd been opening for Slim Dusty (Slim and Joy were also some of Keith's first flag-flyers), and I had lined up after the gig to get his autograph. I also gave him a rock-and-roll guitar-playing Troll doll that I'd bought him to show my appreciation for his music.

Since then, I've watched Keith go on to do so many incredible things (without being a dickhead) in his career and his life (and it's probably not all entirely from the inspiration of the Troll doll …). But he has always remained that beautiful, confident, genuine warm-hearted human who approached me that day at the West Tamworth League Club. I'm fortunate to be able to say that he has supported my music for a long, long time. I am grateful for his friendship, and for what I still consider the best compliment I've ever had in my life.

Sometimes it pays to just not give a shit.

Our musical journey as a job had so far been an equally shared load between our four family members. And when I say 'equally shared', I mean my dad was in charge of most of the driving and the on-stage and off-stage musical duties, while my mum and my brother did all

the booking, management and finances for the band. I actually did … not very much at all. No real life responsibilities, no real interest (yet) in being a part of the music industry, no real motivation to have any actual career in music. Just cruising around, playing songs, having fun and occasionally complaining about nothing, because I had carried some of my stupid, entitled teenager attitude into my early twenties, of course.

But the travelling-family life eventually took a toll on my parents' marriage, which finally ended with a separation and a not-so-surprising finish to The Dead Ringer Band. Despite the divorce, my parents still kept the family unit pretty strong, most of the time.

My mum had spent her whole adult life being Mrs Bill Chambers, but now I watched as she slowly became a fucking boss of a woman who needed no man to give her an identity. But it took some time.

All of my life, I'd seen my mum give. She was just always giving. Sometimes too much, of course, but she also gave a lot just because that's what came from her beautiful, genuine, compassionate heart. She was always caring for and nurturing people around her if she could, and never wanted, needed or took any credit for it. It was never about getting something back. It was always just giving. Quietly, in the background, without attention or fuss. She is basically still living like that now.

Around the time of my parents' separation, we all figured Mum was long overdue to do something for herself. Africa had been on her bucket list forever. But she didn't want to go alone. So she and I set a goal: we would work our butts off for the next year cleaning houses and motel rooms, babysitting, playing cover gigs and saving every penny we earnt until we were able to afford the lowest-budget adventure through Africa together.

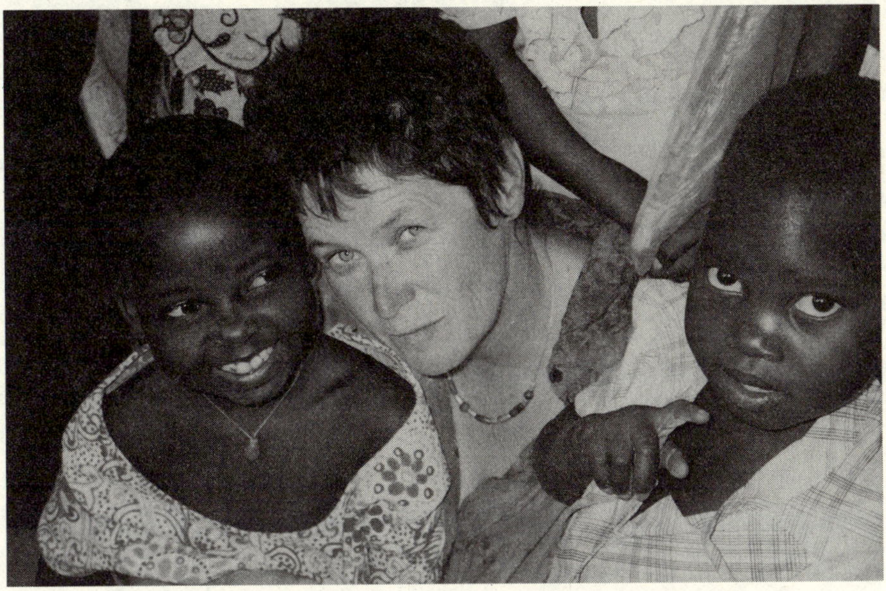

Over the course of five weeks, we travelled through five different countries, staying in self-setting two-man tents, and nothing was ever the same again. Our lives were completely changed by that incredible continent. It felt like it had reached down into our chests, torn off a little piece of our hearts, squeezed it for a bit until it hurt so good, then said, 'I'm gonna keep this now,' and taken it away. Those pieces of our hearts have stayed right there in Africa.

Every single place we went to on that first trip was soul-filling in so many different ways. The landscape, the people, the culture, the animals, the scenery, the children, the history, the lifestyle, the open hearts welcoming us into their beautiful world. I felt a deep connection with this place, like the deep connection I felt to the Australian outback – which actually held a lot of similarities with Africa to me, both visually and through a connection to the land. But while we were travelling around Africa, nowhere else in the world seemed to really exist in my eyes. Mum and I were opening our hearts like we'd never done before as we made our way through South Africa, Zimbabwe, Botswana, Kenya and Tanzania, and even made a visit to Zanzibar Island.

At the start of the trip, I would see all these poor, vulnerable, sometimes orphaned children who seemed to me to have so little in their lives, and barely any opportunity ahead, and my heart would just break for them. I started to feel guilty for having been born into such a privileged place and such a loving family. I had so many possibilities and options ahead in my life. But then I would see my mum with these children. Her connection with them. She so naturally turned our privilege into something so special for so many other people. Instead of feeling guilty, she would use our privilege to give to others.

She would attentively interact with every child like they were her own, always leading with love and compassion. Never with hierarchy or pity. She was so present with every child, feeding them, hugging them, playing with them, loving them. She had this beautiful way of making every single child feel so special. Not because she felt guilty or sorry for them. Just because they *were* special. And she knew how to show them that. Their faces would light up just being around her.

And it wasn't just the kids. She was like that with everyone. She would help the village women make and serve their food, tell them how beautiful they were, and help them hang out their washing and sweep their mud floors.

Yes, even my mum's idea of giving to herself ended up being more about giving to others. Because, in giving, Mum felt like she also received. Whenever she gave with an open heart, she was given an open heart in return.

Seeing my mum, with her open and generous heart, I realised that we really don't need money or material things to be able to make a difference in other people's lives. We can always just do it with love.

I always have something to give.

I had never learnt to speak another language aside from English (and even that is debatable), but it was during this trip that I started to realise that there might have been another reason that my higher old mate had given me this gift of music. Because this special form of communication that I had was actually breaking language barriers right before my eyes, here on the other side of the world from my home.

Every day on our African journey, I would get out my guitar. Sometimes, we'd visit local schools and small villages, and we'd all swap songs from our different cultures. Around the campfire, I would also sing to the local guides and the safari group. Then, while I played guitar, others in the group would sing their songs in their languages and from their countries. Some of the time we couldn't even understand what we were singing about to each other, but it really didn't matter. Our hearts were all connecting through music. We were all communicating with each other. I was starting to see that I had a way to bring people together, through love and music.

Everyone speaks the language of music.

I returned from Africa with a different outlook on life. No longer the spoilt little know-it-all just coasting along while her parents and brother did all the heavy lifting. I felt gratitude. Inspiration. Thankfulness. And I was ready to bring more people together through music.

I think my inner foghorn was trying to tell me that the gift of music that I had been given wasn't just for me. It was time to share it.

After we returned, Mum and I started finding ways through charities, fundraisers and musical visits to help raise money and lift spirits for different people and families all around Australia. And I even brought home a few new songs that would eventually end up on my debut album. One, 'Mr Baylis', I wrote for my safari truck driver, Bill Baylis, on his birthday. There was also 'Don't Talk Back' and 'You Got the Car'. I carried them home and added them to a pile of songs I'd written through my teenage years – 'Cry Like a Baby', 'Don't Go', 'The Hard Way', 'Last Hard Bible', 'Southern Kind of Life' and 'We're All Gonna Die Someday'.

Now there were pieces of my heart in several places, and they all began to feel like home to me in different ways. My hometown of Southend, by the sea. The outback. The continent of Africa. And Norfolk Island, which we had visited for the first time a few years earlier as The Dead Ringer Band. We'd gone for a small country music festival, and instantly found a beautiful connection to the place, and ended up revisiting and even living there on and off for a while. It was also the place where I eventually chose to record my first-ever solo record. I had saved up a few more songs inspired by my love and connection to the island, including 'These Pines', 'This Flower' and a song about my beautiful islander friend, 'The Captain'.

All of these songs meant so much to me. These songs had a special place in my heart and each of them had told me that they needed to be heard. Well, they must have told my inner foghorn, because she's the one who told me about it: 'Kase, you need to share these songs.'

I was ready to record my first solo album. To share these songs with as many people as I could. To embark on a soul-filling solo career, and maybe – my biggest inspiration of all – avoid having to actually get a day job.

It was time.

There is a song in everything.

Supporting others will never take away from who I am. It will only enhance it.

5.

Find your tribe

From this point, it became such a significant part of my journey to be surrounded by people who truly understood who I was and what my musical intention was. Now, at forty-eight years of age, I guess it makes perfect sense – if you surround yourself with negative people who don't believe in you, it's easy to lose belief in yourself, but when you surround yourself with positive people who do believe in you, you're much more likely to feel strong, capable and worthy. But in my early twenties I'm not sure I really thought consciously about any of that kind of stuff.

My dickhead foghorn is (unsurprisingly) not that great at choosing a tribe, but luckily, around the time I was making my first album, I unconsciously gave my wise inner foghorn the job instead. She'd already given my mum and dad a lifetime membership, so she was doing OK so far. I think at that point she really only had one stipulation: my tribe needed to consist of people I could just be myself around. Warts and all. My true self.

Let your inner foghorn choose your tribe.

No one fit the bill more than Nash, of course. He was obviously my big brother, but we had also developed a strong friendship over the years, one that went far beyond family.

Even though the two of us are quite different in personality, we grew up with the same unique life experiences, so we have a special, unwavering bond. Don't get me wrong, we've had our typical brother-and-sister moments too, and sometimes we've fought like cats and dogs, yelling at each other just like when we were kids arguing over a cubbyhouse on the Nullarbor, but it's never lasted that long. We've always had each other's back at the end of the day.

Nash eventually took on the role as my producer and manager, and he went on to work extremely hard at helping to make my solo career everything it became. But he never failed to remind me, the whole way through, that he always cared more about his little sister than he did about the career, the money, the reputation or anything involved in our working relationship together.

He also went on to make his own mark as a successful producer, engineer and studio owner. And as a successful dad of his four awesome kids, too.

A straight-to-the-point, no-bullshit kind of guy with a generous heart (that he tries to pretend he doesn't have), my brother is a rare bird and the most patient person I know.

• • •

My lifelong best friend, roadie and lighting guy is Worm. Arguably the greatest human on earth.

Worm and I have been pretty much inseparable since the day in 1989 when we met. From that moment, he became the fifth member of our family. He travelled with us for most of The Dead Ringer Band's touring days, lived with us on Norfolk Island, co-wrote some of my first-ever and best songs (even though he's not musical at all), squeezed into that four-wheel drive with us, slept in swags with us, took no pay when the gig fees didn't cover our expenses, stood in line with me for Keith Urban's autograph, taught me to smoke cigarettes behind the ag shed at high school, and lugged all our music gear and set our PA system up in every gig all over Australia.

A tough-looking, tattooed, hard-working, beer-drinking bloke with a heart of gold, he can barely manage a sentence without using the word 'fuck', 'shit' or 'cunt', even when he's trying not to.

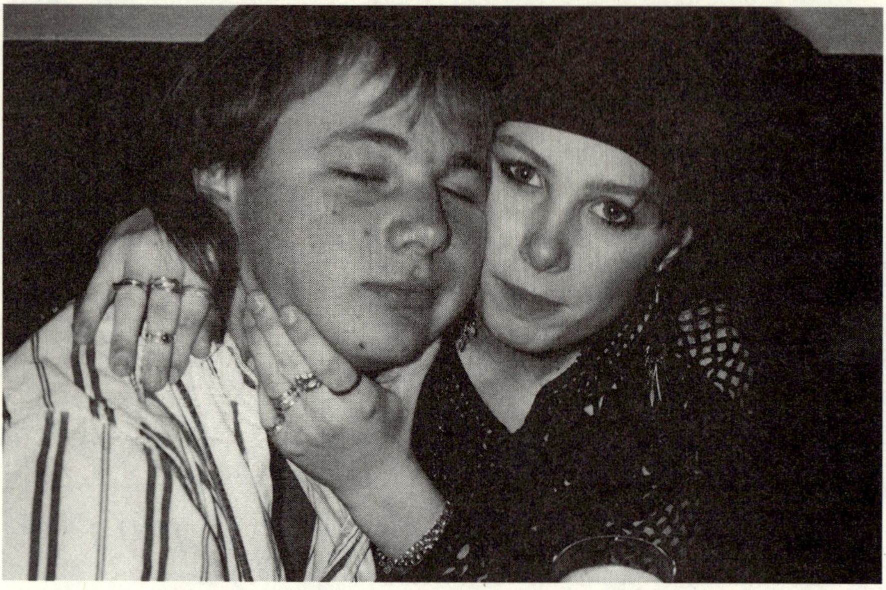

We've travelled the world together. We've eaten out of rubbish bins while drunk in Nashville, Tennessee. I've seen him hand out thirteen cheeseburgers to homeless people in New York City.

I stood next to him at his wedding as his 'best man'. He stood next to me at my wedding as my 'mate of honour'. He stood next to me at my divorce. Our kids are all growing up now as best friends together too.

Almost every day for twenty years, we dragged a VHS player to every hotel room we visited on tour in Australia just so we could watch *Seinfeld* together. When we were in western New South Wales on tour, I had to go pick him up from the police station after he got locked up for the night. He once locked himself out of a hotel room in Canberra in just his old hole-filled undies, and had to walk to reception to ask for another key, which he was refused because he couldn't produce photo ID. All while a busload of tourists waited in line behind him to check in.

I proudly watched him do lights for his favourite artist, Steve Earle.

In the Royal Albert Hall in London, during a Nanci Griffith and London Symphony Orchestra concert performance, I sat next to him while he loudly opened a snuck-in longneck beer and caused the entire room – including those on stage and in the orchestra pit – to glare judgingly in our direction.

When he once accidentally broke into someone's house, drunkenly thinking it was his own, he ended up being invited in for a beer, food and a jam. He played the triangle.

He piggybacked me five kilometres all the way back to our campsite after my first-ever Golden Guitar win because my feet had blisters from wearing heels for the first time.

He joined me on stage uninvited one time to drunkenly introduce one of my songs, only to remember when he saw the audience that he gets stage fright. He wasn't able to say anything else but, 'I did lights for Steve Earle once!'

I once watched him share an entire jumbo packet of chips with a wild possum at 3 am. I've also seen him get bitten by an angry wild baby penguin after saving it from being trapped in a rock cave while we were diving for abalone together.

No matter what the situation is, no matter who he is around, Worm is always just himself. Never pretending to be something he is not. And I am always happy to be around that guy.

• • •

I first met Beccy Sturtzel back when I was thirteen years old, through our family friend and fellow musician Trev Warner. We would visit Trev's house regularly for big musical jams with him and his son

Kym, and one night I walked into their music room and there was this young teenage girl sitting there singing a Dolly Parton song. It was the most beautiful sound I had ever heard.

Before that, I had never really heard a girl my age singing country music at all. Most of my friends liked the pop music that was played on the radio. And I liked that too, but something in my heart always came alive when I heard voices like Emmylou Harris, Tanya Tucker, Loretta Lynn and Dolly Parton.

I watched Beccy sing the rest of that song in awe of her strong, heartfelt, effortless tone, and then I was introduced to her. *Wow. She's nice too! She's so amazing …* I was kinda nervous, as though I was meeting one of my biggest female country music influences – and later Beccy would make that statement true. I would write my first-ever song about her, in honour of our friendship. It was simply called 'Beccy', and I wrote it after we both saw Lucinda Williams in concert for the first time in 1991.

She joined The Dead Ringer Band for a while, and travelled around Australia with us. We would stay up all night as teenagers, talking about boys. We would write songs together. She would change her name to Beccy Cole, and start her successful solo career. I would sing and stand beside her as matron of honour at her wedding. I would hold her baby boy in my arms in the hospital just hours after he was born. I would stand next to her at her divorce. She would nervously open up to me one day to tell me she's gay, and then we would stay up all night talking about girls.

We have sung country songs together on stages all over the world. She once snuck a vibrator into my make-up bag just before I caught a plane to Perth, and the security guard took it out, waved it around and questioned what it was in front of everyone in the line. (Luckily, I'd had Worm carry my bag that day.)

Beccy and I have been through a lot, and we know way too many secrets about each other to ever have the choice to stop being friends.

Find your inner tribe.

The music industry is sometimes portrayed as brutal, cut-throat, scathing and shallow. A place where big corporate companies and greedy businessmen suck the life out of a sacred art form and take advantage while selling the souls of vulnerable and innocent creatives.

Nah. It's not.

Not always, anyway.

OK, obviously there is an element of that in the music industry. There's probably an element of that in every industry, but it doesn't have to be *all* like that. And, sure, it's wise to be aware of that side of music existing, and to be on the look-out for it.

But it's probably pretty safe to say that there has never been a more naive, inexperienced, unaware-of-the-music-industry little singer than I was going into my first solo album experience. And I'm actually extremely grateful for that naivety. If I'd known all the bullshit rules, regulations, restrictions, protocols, requirements, boundaries, demands, orders, dangers, risks and strict formulas that I should have, supposedly, abided by in order to be a 'successful' artist in the music industry, I never would have signed up. But, as naive and inexperienced as I was, looking back I realise now that I always had a secret weapon with me.

No. Not Worm.

My inner foghorn.

And a bit of luck maybe. (Or what I tend to call luck: help from my higher old mate.)

Find your working tribe.

My first proper professional meeting with a major-label record company was with Tony Harlow, the then managing director of EMI Records in Australia.

My mum, dad and brother were all thankfully very keen to still help out with my solo career, so all four of us were directed by a receptionist into Tony's private office in the most stylish, expensive and fancy building, right in the middle of Sydney, I had ever been in before. I was fucking nervous. We all were.

Tony was younger than I thought he would be, but he still looked very intimidating and scary. But he just welcomed us in casually, told us all to take a seat wherever we wanted and started chatting away about actual music in his natural British accent. He talked about his love for Emmylou Harris, Neil Young and Gram Parsons, and within five minutes I felt like myself again. I had calmed down, lost the nerves and was chatting away with Tony like he was a long-lost friend.

It felt real. Genuine. Natural.

The vibe in the room was that we were all exactly where we were supposed to be.

Nothing much was decided on paper that day, as we still had some meetings with other record labels to go to, but my inner foghorn had already told me I had found the home for my debut solo record. If someone else had offered me twice as much money and more promises, I still would have chosen Tony and EMI as my home. Something just felt right.

As we were leaving, Nash asked, 'If we were to start working with you guys, what kind of album do you see Kasey making for her debut record?'

Tony said, 'You guys just make the best album you can. I will find an audience for her. I don't mind what genre it is, I will create a home for her music. It might take me five years, it might take me twenty years, but I'll do everything I can.'

My inner foghorn gave me the thumbs up.

Something really special was created in the room that day. A relationship based on all the things that meant the most to me: connection, freedom, respect, belief, family, trust.

This was the start of my solo career. I signed with Tony Harlow and EMI Records. We made the best album we could. *The Captain*. He found an audience for it. He created a home for it.

And it didn't take twenty years. It didn't even take five years. We hit three times platinum on that first album within two years, then seven times platinum with the next album, *Barricades & Brickwalls*, within five years. The two albums after that – also through EMI – went four times platinum between them. All together, during my time with EMI Records and with four different albums, we celebrated fourteen times platinum.

And, even though Tony and I don't officially work together anymore and now live in different countries, he is still one of my best friends. We talk all the time. With open hearts and the same connection we created in that first meeting. I still send him my newly written songs and ask him for advice, and we still share so much of our lives to this day.

• • •

Around this time I also met a woman who I would look up to as a role model, friend, mother, risk-taker, entrepreneur, mentor and beautiful co-worker for the next thirty years of my life and career: Melita Hodge.

She was working successfully for EMI Records at the time that I first signed with them, and she had a huge hand in creating the success of my albums *The Captain* and *Barricades & Brickwalls*.

She had this incredibly calming and capable energy about her that always reassured me. Every time I was in a room with her, I just felt like everything was gonna be alright. I felt that I was in good hands.

We connected. A real connection.

Melita was smart and kind. Patient and genuine. Wise and

motivated. Open and encouraging. Supportive and passionate. Understanding and honest.

I just loved working with her. I loved being around her. I loved taking advice from her. I couldn't think of anyone else I would rather have representing me as an artist, so when she eventually chose a time to move on from the EMI team we snapped her up to be my manager, alongside my brother.

She still manages my career with my brother to this day. And she's still that same strong, level-headed, kind and inspiring woman she has always been every day since the *Captain* signing.

The combination of my inner foghorn and my higher old mate is the best career supervisor.

If you act like a dickhead, you'll attract dickheads.

6.

Be your own captain

By this point, Norfolk Island had become a second home to me. My mum, Worm and I would travel out there in between most tours. Being almost completely off-grid from the mainland while on Norfolk meant we were easily able to switch off from mainstream society whenever we were there, which always suited me quite well.

It was the place where I felt most grounded, and there was no better place for me to record and bring my first songs to life. So we somehow managed to convince Tony and EMI to put their money towards helping us fly a makeshift studio out to the isolated five-by-eight-kilometre island in the middle of the South Pacific, between Australia and New Zealand. And, as well as taking on the role of my manager, Nash also became my record producer. Which was a direction he was way more interested in anyway.

I guess I thought it must have been really normal for record labels to just trust in their new artist signings and their vision this much. I thought all labels just let artists do whatever it took to honour our creative desires in order to fulfil our artistic needs. I had no idea that it was (and is) extremely rare for a new artist to have been given this much creative freedom, artistic trust and financial support to back it up from a major record label on a first-ever album.

We lived on the island with family friends, and set up our recording studio in an old, unused restaurant next door to their place. I'd written the song 'The Captain' there a couple of years earlier, and I'd known straight away that the song would be a part of me forever. I still remember so clearly the moment when I wrote it. I opened the door to my creative home, and the song just fell out. It was like when you open a door and someone's leaning on the other side of it and they just fall through. That someone was 'The Captain'. I think I felt more like me in that moment than I ever had before. I couldn't really explain it at the time, but it felt like my soul had created this long-lost friend in a song to live with me, in my heart, forever. A song that would always be there for me. A song that would always ground me and make me feel safe. A song that would go on to mean so many different things to me throughout my whole life.

I also knew straight away that it was going to be the title of my first album. I could already see it. I could already feel it. *The Captain* was coming to life.

And the whole album did come to life just a few hundred metres away from where I'd written that song. It came to life with heart, soul, tears, laughter, arguments, love, food and friends. With Worm, Nash and Mum, Dad on guitar, Jeff McCormack on bass and BJ Barker on drums. And with a lot of help from all the Norfolk Island locals.

APRIL - / MAY
97

③

I have handed all my efforts in
Searched here for my second wind
Is there someone here
~~Asked around~~ to let me in ~~Somewhere~~.
~~[illegible] ended up with [illegible] again~~

②

I will have to learn to stand my ground
Ill tell em I wont be around.
~~Ill~~ move on over to your town and hide.

Chorus
And you be the Captain
And Ill be no-one
And you can carry me away if you want to
And you can lay low
Just like your father
And if I tread upon your feet you just say so
Cause your the Captain I am no-one
~~And~~ tend to feel as though I owe one to you.

①

I dont have as many friends because
Im not as pretty as I was
Kicked myself at times because Ive lied

④

So I slammed the doors they slammed at me
found the place Im meant to be.
figured out my destiny At last.

Did I forget to thank you for the ride
I hadnt tried I tend to runaway and hide

My heart was full. Through the whole experience.

My heart still fills up when I think about making that record.

I still play so many of the songs from that record every night on stage.

And my most favourite song I've ever written remains 'The Captain'.

• • •

A month or so after the Norfolk recording, when I had most of the album made, with only a few finishing touches to go, Nash and I went in to have another meeting at EMI Records in Sydney. We were meeting with Tony again, but this time all of the label's Sydney staff would be there too.

It was one of the first actual meetings I'd had with everyone at the Sydney branch, and I was pretty nervous. I had really liked Tony on our first meeting, of course, but at this point I still didn't know him very well. And then there were going to be all these other people there too. People who I'd never even met. All sitting around a big corporate table, making major decisions about my little baby album, which I had created with my family and friends in a run-down old restaurant out at sea.

In the reception area, Nash and I sat there waiting, just like Jerry and George in that *Seinfeld* episode where they go to pitch the TV series to some NBC executives. Nash, so casual and confident like Jerry. Me, so nervous and agitated like George. I wanted to change my mind, just like George, and scream, 'I can't do this! I can't do this!' I wanted to run a mile because the room might be filled with suits and ties and people with secretaries. In that episode, Jerry eventually calms George down by telling him not to worry, they are just TV executives … and just thinking about it actually calmed me down a little. I was ready to go in.

In the meeting, as plans, ideas and album-release schedule dates were thrown back and forth across the table, Nash happily took the reins and I didn't say much. Everyone was talking about radio edits, charting release dates, single plans, video clips, promo budgets, promo tours, album artwork, photo shoots, CD packaging … and my head was fucking spinning! I had never really thought much about any of that stuff. I didn't even know what half of it was. So, feeling out of my depth, I sat back and let the professionals take the lead.

Then someone said, 'OK, let's chat about the name of the album.'

Happy to finally be able to contribute, I spoke up. 'The album is called *The Captain*,' I said.

'Yeah, that's one option,' he replied, 'but let's all throw around some more ideas, and see where we end up.'

My inner foghorn popped up.

I sat there nervously, trying so hard to push her away and just smile while my little heart's dream – the album title that meant so much to me – was about to get pushed away by more intelligent, more experienced, scary people.

But my inner foghorn was not having it. She opened my mouth for me, and I quietly said, 'It's called *The Captain*, guys. It's the song that holds the whole album together. The moment I wrote that song, I knew that's what my first-ever album would be called. Sorry, but that *is* the name.'

My heart started racing. Preparing for the backlash that was undoubtedly about to come at me, I started trying to figure out what else I should put in my closing argument that would shut down this awkward conversation and hopefully give me a way to still be heard …

Then Tony said, 'OK. No problem. *The Captain* it is.'

And the not-so-scary-anymore table full of people who would soon become my beautiful musical team moved on to another topic.

'See,' said my little inner foghorn. 'It's not that hard.'

Being strong doesn't make you a bitch. And being a bitch doesn't make you strong.

As I mentioned, we had a few finishing touches to put on *The Captain* before it was sent in for mixing and mastering. And those finishing touches happened in … Nashville, Tennessee! How fucking cool! To get to work in an actual recording studio, in the birthplace of country music, with one of my favourite guitar players of all time, Buddy Miller. I had been lucky enough to be Buddy's back-up singer at the Byron Bay Bluesfest the year before, with him and his band – Kelley Looney on bass and my favourite drummer, Brady Blade, who would eventually play on my album *Backbone* twenty-six years later. Buddy's usual harmony singer and beautiful wife Julie Miller (also one of my favourite singers) had been unable to come out on tour to Australia with him, so I'd gotten the job. I sang my little heart out in his band, and I even got another gig out of it, singing a duet with Steve Earle (yet another of my favourite artists). Afterwards, my heart was beaming, and Buddy offered his guitar-playing services any time I was in Nashville.

Now, it's not like country singers from the Nullarbor are often just 'in Nashville', so with the help of Tony and EMI we made a special trip to the States so that Buddy could play and sing on a few tracks on my album. Then, just to top it all off, Julie sang a harmony on the song 'The Captain' – that still remains one of the highlights of my entire life.

Once we were done, Buddy offered to take us all out for dinner to celebrate the end of making my debut album. Down the road at his favourite Chinese restaurant, I sat at the table while the waitress put a fortune cookie in front of each of us. I looked around, contemplating my life and how I had ended up in this incredible situation. Here I was, in Nashville, Tennessee. I had just finished recording my first-ever solo record with a major-label record company, in a studio at Buddy Miller's house, with two of my favourite artists in the whole world. They had given their time and their talents to the heartfelt little songs I had saved up throughout my life, songs I was now about to release into the world and begin my musical journey.

This was a life-changing moment. I could feel it. And I knew that, whatever this fortune cookie had to say to me, I would carry it with me forever as inspiration.

I opened up the cookie and read:

You love Chinese food.

OK, not quite as profound as I was hoping for.

But, not willing to give up on the inspirational quote that my higher old mate and this cookie had given me, I decided I would take it to mean that we don't always have to be profound to be inspiring. We only have to be real. And true.

And that my fortune was. Real and true.

I *do* love Chinese food.

We don't have to be profound to be inspiring.

A lot of the time at this point, my music world and my personal world blended together. I didn't really ever draw a line between the two of them too much. I would just wander around from one world to the other, taking each day as it came. My tribe keeping me grounded for the most part whenever I started to get my head up in the clouds and got a bit caught up in all the fuss.

Throughout all the adventures, Worm was always walking beside me, lugging gear and drinking beer. My family was always supporting me and working hard, with Mum taking over the business of merchandise on the road, Dad playing guitar in my band, and Nash managing me and producing all my recordings through every step.

And Beccy had also started her own solo career by this time, so we both had exciting things going on simultaneously and were able to share that along the way. She'd also been through marriage, become a mother and then gotten divorced, so she had plenty of inspiration to write great country songs.

Around this time, she got booked to open a tour throughout New South Wales for Australian country singer Troy Cassar-Daley. Her son, Ricky, wasn't even one year old yet, and she was freshly separated from her husband. Touring with a newborn was looking a little different from normal, so I offered to come out on the road with her as babysitter and to help out during the tour. Of course, I wanted to help out my friend in her time of need – but also being paid in free tickets to see Troy Cassar-Daley play every night was a pretty sweet deal!

I'd heard Troy's music a fair bit over the years, and we had first met in the beer garden at the Brunswick Hotel in Brunswick Heads on the northern New South Wales coast, back in about 1992. Our family band had played at that pub many times, and it had become

one of our favourite regular gigs to play on tour. It was always packed with a great local audience who loved music, and the venue always paid us a good fee and gave us a night's accommodation in the rooms upstairs, a good feed and a few free soft drinks. It was the dream gig for a travelling country band.

Whenever we were booked there, we would roll into town a day before our gig, just to hear the other live bands that the pub had playing. One Saturday night, my whole family wandered into the beer garden, drawn towards this beautiful, unusual voice. It was full and strong, heartfelt and vulnerable. And singing our favourite country songs. This was my kinda singer.

We hadn't heard many country singers on our travels at that point. A lot of pop and rock-and-roll bands played in most of the towns. And I'd certainly never heard a voice quite like this one. This young Aboriginal man from the Gumbaynggirr/Bundjalung tribe was up there singing all the old American country classics by Merle

Haggard and Hank Williams – the songs I had grown up with – but with this unique Australian sound that was so original and different. His sound, which could grab your soul and squeeze it hard in all the right ways, had stolen our hearts. I dreamed that I would one day get to know the beautiful man behind the voice.

From then on, our paths crossed a little bit at festivals, club gigs and pubs all around Australia. I loved Troy's music and got a true, natural gentlemanly vibe from him on stage. And I always held on to the hope that we'd get to know each other one day, so when this tour with Beccy came up I thought it might be my chance. Maybe at last, while backstage, I'd get to know the real Troy, the man who I had looked up to as an inspiring singer/songwriter for all this time.

• • •

It was the opening night of the tour, and even though I was very used to being backstage I knew my place was a little different this time. My role was one of babysitter, so I had to keep Ricky close to his mama for his regular breastfeeds but also try to stay out of the way as much as I could and not cramp anyone's style.

On stage, I had always found Troy to be so welcoming and friendly but also a little more self-composed and poised than I was generally used to. So, I had decided that I was to be on my most well-mannered and best behaviour. I wanted to make a good impression on this seasoned, mature and dignified musician. With baby on hip, I quietly entered the backstage dressing room, ready to politely reintroduce myself.

Instead, I was greeted with a room full of musicians all cheering on a grown man who was sitting awkwardly on the floor in their midst, with a look of the most pure concentration and determination.

Facing the group, he had his legs in the air, a cigarette lighter in his hand and his neck hunched over. Trying to light up his own fart.

Then a loud noise erupted, and the gas from Troy's arse lit up the entire room.

Everyone applauded, celebrated, while a slight rise in the upper lip and a head-nod from Troy showed the pride and accomplishment he genuinely felt deep down.

Then he turned to me and said, 'Kase! Come in, mate!'

I decided I liked this guy more than ever.

My best behaviour was no longer needed, and we've been beautiful friends ever since.

Dream out loud.

My journey throughout *The Captain* years was filled with life-changing experiences and unique memories, but I didn't always know quite what was happening at the time.

When the album was about to be released, I was invited to play at the EMI Records annual conference, as their new artist signing. It was being held at a ritzy hotel resort in tropical North Queensland, and I was very excited. I'd never been to a hotel this fancy before. They even had a bar in the pool! What the fuck? And the label had paid for my flights there *and* back! So cool.

My end of the deal was to acoustically showcase a couple of songs from *The Captain* to EMI staff from all around Australia. I had never played any of my songs live to all the staff before, and luckily I didn't really know what a big deal that was – otherwise, I probably would have been shitting myself.

A few months earlier, I had recorded a few cover songs to feature on B sides of singles throughout the release period. One of those songs was the Crowded House hit 'Better Be Home Soon'. Now, remember I hadn't grown up with much TV, radio or the kind of mainstream marketing and exposure that most kids had, so if I'm honest I wasn't even that sure who Crowded House were. Someone at the label had suggested I cover that song, and I vaguely knew of it and liked the beautiful melody, so it seemed like a good fit.

As I was sound-checking in the function room of the resort ahead of my short performance, an EMI staff member asked whether I was going to play it. 'I actually don't know how to play the chords on guitar very well,' I replied right at the exact moment that Neil Finn, the singer of Crowded House and also an EMI-signed artist, walked into the room. Not that I was aware of who he was. I just sat there obliviously, trying to figure out the chords to his song.

Eventually, another EMI staffer introduced me to him and the penny dropped. A little. At the very least, I knew I was being introduced to the writer of the song I was trying to play, so I just blurted out, 'Hey, mate. You know this song. What are you doing later today? Can you play guitar for me?' Due to my extreme naivety and sheltered upbringing, I had no idea that I was standing in the presence of world-famous musical royalty and blatantly asking him to back me up while I sang his own song in front of his long-time record label.

But, if he was at all offended by this request coming from an inexperienced, ignorant, uninformed amateur, he certainly didn't show it. He graciously grabbed his guitar, and we performed the beautiful song together.

And, as quickly as it was born, Neil Finn's brief career as my back-up guitar player for corporate events was over.

Sometimes it's better not to know ...

Not everything fell into place quite as easily as that, though. The first review I ever got for my first solo release was from a street-press paper in Brisbane, Queensland. It was for the debut of my first single 'Cry Like a Baby', and it read, 'And you thought Shania Twain was bad! This song will leave you standing in the corner saying, "Make it stop, please make it stop," as the men in white coats come to cart you away.'

I didn't really know how important reviews were to new artists at the time, plus I had never had anyone write anything about me in a magazine before. So I framed it anyway, and I hung it on my wall.

• • •

Not long after the Australian release of *The Captain* we got a record deal in the UK and Europe with Virgin Records, and in the States with Warner Music. Geez. What a spin-out, hey? I couldn't really believe it.

I wasn't exactly taking the world by storm overnight, and mainstream radio was not about to play a country song no matter who released it, but this little chick from the Nullarbor was being given the chance to share some of her songs in places all around the world. Who'da thunk it?

I did a few little showcases throughout the UK and Europe, mostly to small audiences and people from the record label, and also started travelling to the States to give them a little taste of what an Australian country singer had to say. When I showed up to my first record-store performance in Nashville, Tennessee, one of the store's staff asked me, 'So did you record your album in Australian or in English so we can understand it here too?'

I was starting to realise just how far away Australia was from the rest of the world.

• • •

One night, I was playing a gig to about thirty people in Washington, D.C., when I looked down from the stage and saw this young guy with chains hanging from his leather and denim clothing and the most fiercely spiked pink-and-black hair I had ever seen. He was standing by himself in the front row (the only row, actually – almost everyone else was at the bar) and, since he definitely didn't look like my usual audience member, he stood out a fair bit.

Then I started playing 'These Pines' – my slowest, most heartfelt country ballad from *The Captain* – and he sang passionately along with every word. At this point, not many people in the States even knew who I was, let alone the lyrics to any of my songs. But this guy spent the entire set lost in every lyric and melody, and he was particularly zoned in on my dad's country guitar playing in my band.

What was this young, cool, rock star–looking guy doing at my gig here on the other side of the world?

After the gig, my dad's curiosity got the better of him. He walked up and said, 'Hey, mate. You look a bit outta place here, but thanks for coming. I'm Bill, Kasey's dad.'

'I'm Benji,' the guy replied. 'Great set.'

They got chatting, and Dad invited Benji to join us for a late dinner down the road. We spent the night talking music and sharing touring stories, and learnt that Benji had heard 'The Captain' being played on a random little radio station – an airplay that also apparently later led to the song being played on an episode of *The Sopranos* when it was the number one TV show in the States at the time.

Benji was one of the nicest and most genuine people I had ever met, and his stories ended up being a little more interesting than ours because he was in a band with his twin brother, Joel, and two others. It was called Good Charlotte. Of course, I had never heard of them, but it wasn't long before I was recognising our random lone audience member and dinner companion on TV screens and music-mag covers all over the world.

• • •

I was booked to play my debut single, 'Cry Like a Baby' – the very same one that had been so colourfully reviewed by the street press in Brisbane not long before – on an American TV show. I wasn't quite used to TV appearances at this point, but I was certainly happy enough to show up at *The David Letterman Show* in New York City and play my little country song.

Luckily, I really didn't know what a big deal it was to play on a show like that, otherwise I would have definitely been a lot more nervous than I was. I'd heard of the show of course, and had even seen a few episodes, so I knew it wasn't every day that a young girl from outback Australia who'd learnt to sing country songs around the campfire with her dad was given this opportunity, but I really didn't think that much about it. I was mainly just excited and nervous to be playing on a TV show at all.

I had my *Captain* band with me – my dad on guitar, BJ Barker on drums, Jeff McCormack on the bass and another mate of ours, James Gillard, on rhythm guitar. We'd been travelling a lot together around Australia, doing a fair few gigs, and we were all pretty pumped to go into a real TV studio in New York City.

It was sound-check time. The studio was cold. The staff were nice, helpful and very professional. The sound was great. The house band was very friendly and supportive. But David Letterman was nowhere to be seen.

As we started packing up our things to leave sound-check and find our dressing room before showtime, I noticed my bass player Jeff quietly wandering over to David Letterman's famous chair, which was sitting there empty, waiting for the star to arrive. Jeff quickly and unassumingly sat down in the chair, paused for a moment and, before anyone could tell him to get out, he was back on his feet and shuffling over to Worm and me. Then he leaned over to us and whispered, 'It's not every day you get the opportunity to fart in David Letterman's chair.'

He was right. He was wise to seize that moment. He was never given that opportunity again.

Although, many years later, we would go on to have the opportunity to 'sit' in Jay Leno's chair, and in Conan O'Brien's seat. Twice.

In every empty chair that lies before you there is an opportunity to 'sit' in it.

Not long after our *Letterman* performance, I was lucky enough to be booked to open a tour throughout the States for singer/songwriter Robert Earl Keen. We were all so excited. What an opportunity. A seasoned, heartfelt, prolific American songwriter who we had been inspired by over the years. It would be an honour to play for his audience.

We started the tour down south, and I was (Robert Earl) keen as. Ready to share my sincere, honest lyrics with this beautiful audience who would obviously have the same love and respect for profound songwriters as I did, since we all shared the link of being fans of Robert Earl Keen. What a privilege. I wandered out on stage.

Within the first two songs of my set, the crowd had built up a deafening, ear-bursting chant of epic proportions. Over and over, they screamed, 'ROBERT EARL KEEN! ROBERT EARL KEEN!' at me, and kept it up until our thirty-minute set had ended.

Fuck. I did *not* expect that.

Shocked by this musical fail we'd just experienced, my band and I convinced ourselves it was likely to just be a rare, one-off, extreme occurrence. Tomorrow night in Louisiana would probably be a completely different outcome, we were sure.

But Mardi Gras week in New Orleans proved to be even worse. Along with the chanting throughout every one of our songs, they were also throwing things at us this time, in an attempt to hopefully hurry up our set and move us along to make room for their beloved main act.

Night after night, this same thing occurred, over and over. I was starting to wonder what the hell I'd gotten myself into.

Despite our failing performances, Robert's band and crew made us feel very welcome. And, as the tour wore on, they eventually explained that this happened to every opening act down south for Robert Earl Keen. In fact, they said, we'd already lasted longer on the tour that some bands did. Years later, I would have some fellow musicians tell me they always just said a flat-out 'no' to opening any southern Robert Earl Keen gigs, because they are just too damn hard.

But I was in it for the long haul. And maybe this was handed to me as a test? To see how deep I could dig to win over the unwinnable crowd?

The next gig I was fucking determined, and I took a completely new approach to trying to break through to this crowd: I changed my set list around, I shortened my long stories, I got straight to the point, I only played my up-tempo songs, I ditched the self-indulgent ballads, I lost the polite little girl act (which wasn't really me anyway) and I channelled my loud, commanding voice to cut through the chants. I demanded to be fucking heard!

OK, that didn't really work either.

But fuck I tried hard.

After a while, we headed up north and the crowds got much nicer and way more respectful. I'm glad we stuck it out. Nothing was ever thrown at us again.

Sometimes there's no lesson. Sometimes it's just fucking hard and you have to stick it out.

I went from that tour to opening another one, this time for my biggest female role model in music and the woman who inspired me to write my first song, Lucinda Williams. Five weeks across the United States of America, and these audiences were attentive and beautiful and unlike any I'd ever played to.

I wasn't sure whether I'd actually get the chance to talk to Lucinda at all, not really knowing whether main acts mingled with their opening acts or just kept more to themselves. But, on the first day of the tour, I was sitting on my bus when I heard a knock at the door. I opened it up, and standing there was Lucinda Williams.

Flustered and a little frantic, she said in her southern drawl, 'Can I borrow some nail-polish remover?'

I declared it as the greatest moment of my life.

You never know when nail-polish remover can change your life.

The first time I ever sang with renowned Aussie musician and songwriter Paul Kelly was at the Basement in Sydney. Our family loved Paul's music and we had seen him play in concert a few times. I had met Paul briefly once before the year prior at the Byron Bay Bluesfest, when he walked past the tent I was playing in and heard me covering 'Cripple Creek' by The Band, which prompted him to come up and introduce himself.

This brief meeting was a stepping stone to Paul inviting me to play on stage with him at the Sydney gig. It was a sell-out, soul-filling and incredible. Singing with him gave me equal amounts of heartfelt excitement and nerve-wracking anxiety.

Once the room had emptied after the show was over, we were about to start our trek home when Paul came up to us and invited us to join him in the back bar of the venue for a private after-party.

An after-party? With actual rock stars?

My fear popped straight up and started giving me a very stern warning. 'Kase, you've seen the movies,' it said. 'You've heard the stories. You know what a famous rock-star after-party means. Sex, drugs and rock-and-roll!'

Mmmmmmm … that's not my style at all.

'You know what this is going to be like, Kase,' fear continued. 'Outrageous, reckless drunken behaviour with tables full of hardcore drugs and TVs violently thrown out of hotel windows then cops showing up with batons to shut it all down.'

Nope. I really don't want to be a part of that. I think I should listen to my fear and run a mile …

Paul had already headed off to the after-party, thinking we would follow. But fear and I decided we should decline the invitation. With the intention of quickly popping back in to say, 'Thank you for the offer, Paul, but we have a long drive home,' we tentatively walked into the wild rock-star after-party. My fear was getting ready to walk me straight back out again when we were greeted by Paul, his whole band, his crew and all their family members, huddled together around one little table. They were passing acoustic bluegrass instruments around while singing old gospel hymns in beautiful harmony.

Paul handed a guitar to me and my dad, and asked us to join in. We played and sang along all together, while our hearts filled up even more with some of the most beautiful musical sounds we had ever heard being created around us.

When Paul asked if Dad and I knew any old Louvin Brothers songs, we launched into 'My Baby's Gone' together. Paul grabbed the hand of the lady sitting beside him, whisked her up, and they waltzed gracefully together around the room until our rendition of the 1958 classic was done.

Be still, my beating heart! If this was really what rock-star after-parties were all about, then sign me up.

Don't believe everything you hear.

I then got to open up a tour for Emmylou Harris. Now this was my actual dream come true! I could not believe that I was getting to do this, but I was.

When we were nearly at the end of the tour, I was sitting in my dressing room taking a moment to reflect on this incredible experience. Every night, I'd got to hear my first-ever female musical inspiration sing live in all the major cities of my home country. I'd

had the privilege of playing my own original songs to her beautiful audience before her set each gig. I'd gotten to sing the guest part with Emmylou every night on 'My Baby Needs a Shepherd' – a part that was originally sung by another idol of mine, Patty Griffin. I'd got to hear one of the greatest live bands in the world play, backing her up every night – Buddy Miller on guitar, Tony Hall on bass and my favourite drummer in the world, Brady Blade! I'd personally got to know the incredible band, crew and Emmylou herself over the entire tour. And I'd also watched my dad get up and play the dobro with Buddy Miller in his opening set, while Emmylou played rhythm guitar in the background for them every single night.

This was unbelievable.

I sat there and thought, *There is no greater gift in the world than what I have just been given.*

Then Emmylou popped her head into my dressing room and handed me a wrapped gift for my upcoming twenty-fifth birthday. I opened it. A pair of black-and-silver fishnet stockings. Now THIS was the greatest gift I'd ever been given.

Being proud of myself and my achievements does not make me a dickhead.

Be fucking grateful.

7.

Be brave enough to be vulnerable

My touring life was filled with some incredibly cool random stuff, and I was discovering that playing live and travelling all around was filling up my heart more than I could have ever imagined. But, as much as the gigs and live performing were filling my heart, learning more about the behind-the-scenes of the music industry was actually draining my heart a little.

I was getting to know the rules, regulations and politics that are involved underneath the music. I was starting to understand more about the musical and image-based formula that we are all expected to abide by as artists in order to create 'success' in the music industry. And honestly, it was somewhat discouraging.

There seemed to be so much importance placed on radio airplay, and yet so many boundaries around what actual music ever got a chance of being played on mainstream radio stations in Australia. The amount of sacrifice and tailoring a country singer like me would have had to realistically make and do in order to have had even the slightest shot on mainstream radio was so far from anything that I was doing – or willing to do.

There weren't really many folky, organic-sounding singer/songwriters being played on mainstream radio at all back then, and certainly no country music. The radio charts were dominated by artists like Britney Spears, Christina Aguilera, Shakira and the Spice Girls. I was also a young woman in the music industry, but I felt like that's pretty much where our similarities ended. On one hand, I didn't even really want to be anything like these artists – musically or image-wise – but I was also a young girl, and these were the main female role models that young girls were hearing on the radio, and seeing on the covers of magazines and TV screens. Sometimes, I would hear their songs and see their perfect, sexy bodies dancing around in their music videos, or their beautiful, flawless faces on the magazines covers, and I just felt so … different.

I felt so real. But not 'real' in a good way so much anymore. I felt real and imperfect. I felt honest and flawed. I felt small and plain. I sometimes just felt invisible.

As I'm writing this now, I am trying to remember whether there'd ever been a time before this when I'd ever really, truly felt intimidated by other women. I can't. I think it was around this time in my life, when I was being repeatedly exposed to and so closely involved with mainstream media and social attention, that all my insecurities subtly opened up. It marked the first time in my life that, unfortunately, I really started comparing myself to others.

• • •

One day, I just sat down with my guitar and started singing, 'Am I not pretty enough? Is my heart too broken? Do I cry too much? Am I too outspoken? Don't I make you laugh? Should I try it harder? Why do you see right through me?'

And the chorus to 'Not Pretty Enough' was born.

Both the lyrics and melody had just fallen out so easily. So naturally. So vulnerably.

But the verses were yet to come. I knew the song was special and I had a connection to it instantly, but I also knew I needed to come back and finish it at another time. On another day, with a much stronger, clearer, more self-assured headspace. I had got as open and honest as I was prepared to be at that point.

So, about a week later, I sat down with a solid plan. I knew the chorus was special, but it obviously had a bit too much vulnerability in it. I had to make sure that the verses were different. *Let's even it out a bit*, I thought. *No one wants to hear me waffle on for an entire song with my dumb insecurities and lack of self-confidence, so I at least have to make sure that the verses are not as revealing and exposed as the chorus.*

When I actually thought about it, I didn't even really wanna be like those girls anyway. Those were just my stupid little insecurities, things that only I felt, so I shouldn't really reveal any more than I already had. I had to change the direction of the song. *Let's steer it.*

I tried, and I tried, and I tried.

Over and over.

I came back week after week, attempting the verses and planning the direction of the song.

I thought, and I thought, and I overthought.

Nothing worked. Nothing sounded right. Nothing felt good

enough. Nothing was setting my creative soul on fire. Nothing that I thought people wanted to hear was matching up with what I wanted to say.

That's when I started to wonder if maybe this song was actually *not* meant to be for other people to hear. Maybe it had a different purpose? Maybe my heart just needed to say some things? Some real things. Some vulnerable things. Things I didn't like that I felt within myself and didn't want to share with anyone else.

I sat down with my guitar in hand in exactly the same spot where the chorus had fallen out of me, and I decided that all I needed to do was bring this song to life. I didn't ever actually have to play it to another person if I didn't want to.

Just finish it now and decide that later, I told myself.

Don't write for the listener. Just write for the song.

Write from who I am, not from who I want people to see me as.

Write from my heart.

My little inner foghorn had popped up, and was telling me that it's OK to just be vulnerable. 'Just let go now,' she said. 'Feel how you feel, and leave the other stuff for later.'

When I tuned out of my head and tuned into my heart, when I went back to that same vulnerable place the chorus had fallen from, the verses to 'Not Pretty Enough' finally came to life.

I live, I breathe, I let it rain on me.
I sleep, I wake, I try hard not to break.
I crave, I love, I've waited long enough.
I try as hard as I can.
I laugh, I feel.
I make-believe it's real.

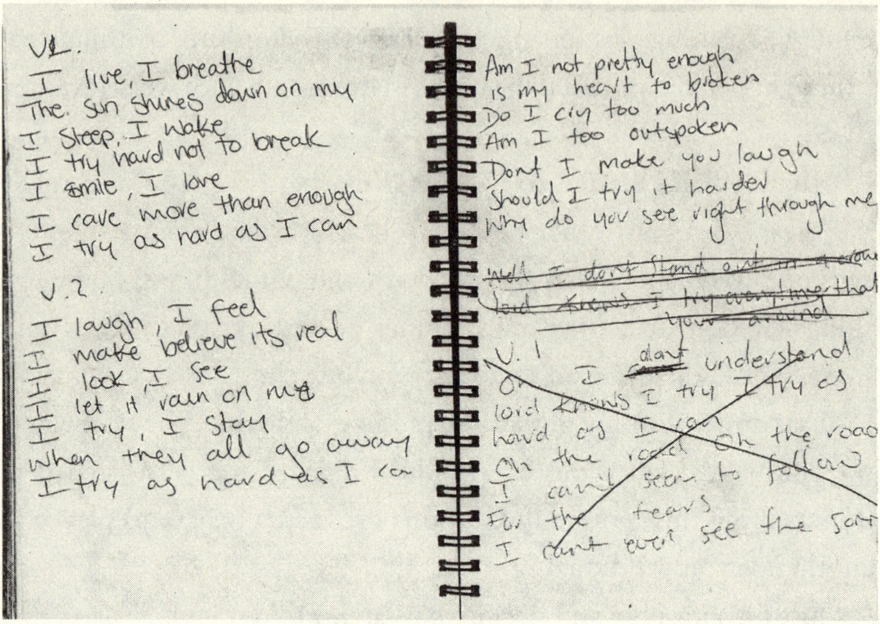

I fall, I freeze.
I pray down on my knees.
I hold, I stand.
I take it like a man.
I try as hard as I can.

I felt everything. All the parts of me. Every weakness and every fear, every doubt and every uncertainty. I let them all come up and take over. The vulnerability that I had tried so hard not to feel anymore and not show was now leading the way.

• • •

'Not Pretty Enough' was the first of my songs that any mainstream radio station ever played. And before too long, they were all playing it. On high rotation. The song went all the way to number one on the mainstream singles chart, became a three-time platinum-selling single, and took my album *Barricades & Brickwalls* to number one on the mainstream albums chart at the same time and to seven times platinum. I was nominated for seven ARIA awards the following year for 'Not Pretty Enough' and *Barricades & Brickwalls*, and won Best Country Album, Best Female Artist and Album of the Year.

There had been a time when I'd thought that sharing too much vulnerability in my songs would hold my music career back, but the thing I once saw as my biggest weakness became my greatest strength.

My life was never the same again.

Be brave enough to be vulnerable.

All of a sudden people on the street knew who I was. It was weird. Not bad. Just weird.

When I walked into a shop in Perth, the lady who served me said, 'You look a lot like that Kasey Chambers chick.'

I laughed a little and was just getting ready to tell her that, actually, I was that chick when she put her hand up to stop me and said, 'Oh, don't worry! You look heaps better than her.'

A backhanded compliment is still a compliment.

Behind all those barricades and brick walls, there was another slightly less poetic inspiration behind this chart-topping album. The person responsible for the album name even existing in the first place. My roadie, Worm.

Not long after I wrote 'Not Pretty Enough', Worm presented my dad and me with an opportunity. 'I've got an idea for a song for ya,' he said with pure confidence. 'You're gonna help me finish writin' it, and then you're gonna fuckin' record it and put it on your next album. OK?'

Dad and I were a bit surprised. Worm wasn't musical in any way. He didn't sing or play any instruments, or even show much interest in the creative side of music. The only other song idea he'd brought to us in the past was 'Oh, how I'd love to be a woman's bicycle seat'. But in this moment he blurted out, 'Barricades and brick walls won't keep me from you.'

Dad and I looked at each other. We couldn't hide how good we thought the line was, and we all started creating the rest of the song 'Barricades & Brickwalls' right then and there.

We finished it.

We loved it.

Worm was right.

And not only did I fuckin' record it, but it became the title track of the record. Worm the roadie had played a crucial part in creating a seven-times-platinum-selling album.

• • •

Many years later, in 2015, I was sitting at a restaurant having dinner one night when my phone started going crazy with a million messages from all these random friends I hadn't heard from in years. Kylie and

Kendall Jenner had just posted a bunch of Snapchat videos in which they were singing my songs. What the fuck?

I knew it must have been some kind of a big deal at the time, but I still had to ask my dinner date who exactly these two random American girls were and what Snapchat was.

Once it was properly explained to me who these famous celebrities were, and why it was so noteworthy that they were singing my songs, the only person I really wanted to share it with was Worm. Of course.

In these posts, Kylie and Kendall had announced that the first album they'd ever owned had been *Barricades & Brickwalls*. I'm sure they speak with the same admiration and appreciation for the similar impact that Worm obviously had on their careers too.

Always listen to Worm.

The success of 'Not Pretty Enough' and *Barricades & Brickwalls* had a snowball effect, and it was all happening right there in front of my eyes. This little song I had written from the deepest place of vulnerability in my heart was now connecting with people all over the world.

My life was turned upside down.

To make things just a little more interesting, I'd also fallen pregnant around the same time. Luckily, I hadn't been told much 'women can't have a career and a baby at the same time' bullshit by many people, so I had no reason to think otherwise. I was over the moon with happiness and ready to juggle the two, with the help of my partner at the time, Cori, and my family. Tony and my label were also extremely supportive of my motherhood venture.

In the music video for 'Not Pretty Enough', the cameras only shot me from the chest up, because we made it when I was seven months pregnant. (Whenever I felt a bit tired, I reminded myself that, at this same stage while pregnant with me, my mum had been siphoning fuel to save her life in a moving car while being shot at by an angry farmer.) It was set at a high-school dance where I was the singer on stage – and eighteen years later, I would sing that same song at my son Talon's high-school dance in his graduating year! Also, if you look really closely in the video, you might recognise a very young Angus and Julia Stone, who played students at the dance. I would proudly watch them go on to become two of Australia's most successful and ground-breaking artists in the years to come.

I started to tour the world a lot more regularly at this point – in tour buses, with a full band, crew, my family and even a tour manager sometimes. I haven't really had a tour manager since, but it was fun for a while. Not long after the 'Not Pretty Enough' video was made, I jumped on a plane and did one last tour in the States before my first baby was due. International flights, driving from town to town, playing gigs most nights, sound-checks, promotional appearances at record stores, radio performances, press interviews and trying to find time to rest while attempting to get on top of the jetlag all while seven months pregnant – in hindsight, it was probably a bit too much to be doing, but I wasn't quite ready to slow down yet.

Near the end of the tour, we took to the stage for our second-to-last show at a place called Bimbo's in San Francisco. I was four songs into the set, singing 'These Pines', when I started to feel a bit dizzy. I think (I can't remember exactly) that I stood back from the microphone, towards my dad, who was on stage playing guitar, and then I collapsed to the ground. Dad said later that he'd seen my eyes starting to roll back in my head and realised I was about to pass out, so he'd grabbed me and cushioned my fall as I struck the stage floor in front of the entire audience. All this is a bit of a blur to me, obviously, but I do kinda remember coming back to consciousness, lying on the floor, with a doctor standing over me. An Australian doctor, actually, who just happened to be in the audience at the time. (Thank you, higher old mate.)

It turned out to be nothing too serious on paper – low blood pressure. More than likely, it was a not-so-subtle way of my body telling me to slow things down a bit. I was pregnant, overworked, under-rested and not looking after myself like I should have been.

I wanted to go back out on stage and finish the gig (yep, I'm a dickhead), but Dad, Nash, the rest of the band and the doctor made an executive decision, outranking me and my poor dickhead judgement.

Instead, we promised we'd return to San Francisco for a make-up show the following year, and everyone in the audience booked back in for it – including the doctor. And even though we offered people their money back at the door, everyone declined as a token of good faith. We also cancelled the last show for the tour, which was scheduled for the next night, and I flew home a few days early to look after myself and my baby.

• • •

My first child, Talon, was born a couple of months later. He was right there with me on the journey of 'Not Pretty Enough'.

Four days ahead of Talon's due date, my waters broke, and four hours later I became a mother for the first time. My life as I knew it had completely changed again. Mostly in a good way. Except for the sleepless nights, the extra laundry, the healing stitches, the howling cries, the cracked nipples, all the extra crap we had to travel with, the baby vomit, the constant bad smells on my clothes, the leaky boobs, the dirty nappies, the extreme fatigue, the extra weight, the emotional meltdowns, the stretch marks, the teething and the embarrassment of my baby's explosive diarrhoea on the crisp white sheets of the fancy Como Hotel next door to the Channel 10 studios on Chapel Street in Melbourne.

It wasn't too long before I was back out on the road with my band and crew, dragging my newborn and my partner all around the world again, and sometimes still ignoring my body's warning signs telling me when to slow down a little.

My body is way smarter than I am.

Embrace change.

8.

Authenticity is the easiest sell

I was backstage at the ARIA Awards when I heard a loud and iconic Aussie accent scream at me, 'I AM SOOOOOO NOT PRETTY ENOUGH!'

It was none other than Australian legend Steve Irwin. The Crocodile Hunter himself was there, talking to me, with a giant python wrapped round his neck.

I had dreamt about this moment for a long time. And fortunately, I'd had such faith it would one day randomly occur that I was prepared. I immediately took my limited-edition 'Steve Irwin, Crocodile Hunter' miniature figurine out of my handbag (complete with attached Sharpie) and got him to autograph it right then and there. I didn't stop smiling for the rest of the night.

I guess you could say I was getting into the habit of over-preparing,

but I would also soon realise it was just as important to teach myself to let go. I started noticing that everything flowed a lot better for me in a gig (and in general life) if I prepared really well beforehand – by doing little things like writing set lists, having fresh strings on my guitar and fresh batteries in my tuner, learning my songs well enough, doing a decent sound-check – and then, knowing I'd done everything within my control, when it came time to play the actual gig I just trusted and let go.

Every gig had a life of its own. Every audience was different. Every person in the audience was having their own intimate journey throughout the performance. And if I could let go and be completely lost in the moment, then every gig would be special in its own way for me as well. So I would over-prepare ... then let every gig just sweep me up in its own magic. I sang a lot of the same songs each night, and even told some of the same stories about each one, but when I truly let go every gig felt new and unique. Like its own adventure.

For the most part, I've carried this approach into the rest of my life too. Recording albums, I get very prepared, then when the time comes to let the magic take over, I let go and just enjoy the ride.

Travelling, I pack everything I might possibly need – extra toothbrush, first-aid kit, eight pairs of shoes for a four-day trip – but when flights are inevitably delayed or the road is closed I go with the flow and make the most of the new plan. And we usually still make the gig.

Grocery shopping, I always have an extensive grocery list written out, but if I get to the shop and they've run out of toilet paper I know I also have my emergency stash at home that I prepared earlier. So, when the time comes, I can really let go.

Crikey, it's good to be prepared ... then let go.

After my third solo album, *Wayward Angel*, won me Best Female Artist at the 2004 ARIA Awards, I was busy on the promo trail, doing interviews and performances with all sorts of TV, radio and press to celebrate and use my win. I was getting pretty used to this lifestyle by then. Confidently walking in and out of radio and TV stations like a total pro.

One day, en route to meet another journalist at another fancy cafe, I remembered I had to pick up a prescription from my family doctor. He'd left it with the receptionist, so I would be able to run in and quickly grab it on my way.

It turned out Dr Norrie had also left me a note:

Dear Kasey,

Congratulations on your ARIA award. We are all proud of you.

P.S. Your pap smear is overdue.

There's nothing like an invasive vaginal swipe to bring you back down to earth.

Most of the interviews and performances I did publicly, I really enjoyed. I felt swept up in them just like my gigs. I was fairly comfortable opening up and giving my true self, and would mostly just answer honestly. Whoever I was talking with or performing to, I always got lost in the moment and mostly found it pretty easy to just let the experience flow naturally.

Walking away from most interviews and public appearances, I'd feel happy with how they'd gone. Even if I'd messed up the chords a little, sung a wrong lyric here or there, or said something silly, I didn't really mind. It was all just part of being who I was. Not overthinking anything too much. Just letting it be what it is.

But then I started noticing that, when I watched things back or read the articles or listened to the interviews, I would start picking things apart about myself, criticising things that I'd done or the way I'd done them. And it wasn't exactly a healthy critique, either. I started looking for things to not like about myself.

Why do I close my eyes when I sing? Why do I pull those weird faces? Why do I have to answer questions so honestly? Why do I laugh so loud? Why do I reveal so much of myself to complete strangers in interviews? Why do I look so serious in sad songs? Why do I wear my hair like that?

Why do I hold my guitar on an angle? Why don't I think more before I say things? Why didn't I put more make-up on?

All this even though, when I'd left the interview, I'd felt great. Happy to have given my true, imperfect self. I hadn't really cared about any of that other stuff.

It was starting to feel like the vulnerable things that I sometimes felt – and put into my songs – were only really magnified when I watched, read or heard anything about myself. It was only when I looked back at myself through other people's eyes.

My own eyes didn't really mind my imperfections.

• • •

A few days after the ARIA promo trail, I read a wrap-up of the ARIA Awards where the journalist compared the way that I'd walked into the backstage press-conference room after my win with the way that Kylie Minogue did the same thing. Needless to say, my way was a little less poised, refined and experienced than Kylie's. And hers was a little less daggy, fumbly and like a deer caught in the headlights than mine.

It started to feel like, every time I read or watched something about myself, I handed my self-confidence and self-assurance over to someone else – and then they found a way to dig into my smallest, deepest insecurities and open them up to make them feel huge!

The weird thing was that most of the press and public attention I was getting was actually quite positive and supportive. Even the Kylie comparison – it was written in a way that highlighted the endearing qualities of my win. But I guess the funny thing about insecurities is that we have a clever way of making them feel bigger than they really need to be: we scrutinise ourselves through other people's eyes instead of accepting ourselves through our own.

It still hadn't quite sunk in that my weaknesses and imperfections were actually my strengths. But it was during this time that I started to realise that, as well as letting go in the moment, it was probably just as important for me to learn to leave things in the moment as well. I continued to fulfil all of the promotional duties that came with the job, and I gave my true and imperfect self at the time, but I decided to leave the beautiful memory of each experience as just that. A memory.

I stopped reading or watching or listening to much of it afterwards. Stopped searching out reviews, listening back to interviews, revisiting TV performances. Instead, I made some peace with my imperfections. I decided if I had given my true self in the moment, then that was always more than enough.

People can judge me, but I get to decide whether or not I'm going to feel judged.

Being a mum and having a career was working quite well in harmony most of the time. Then, when Talon was about two years old, I fell pregnant again. Cori and I were over the moon with happiness.

It felt amazing to be pregnant again. Cori and I were very much in love and ready to have another child, and I had loved being pregnant the first time, so knowing there was another baby growing inside me filled my heart with joy. We started picking out names, daydreaming about the possibility of a girl or a boy, buying more baby clothes and sharing our beautiful news with some of our immediate family.

A few days away from our twelve-week scan, just as we were getting ready to tell everyone else, I went to pee and noticed some blood. I'd had a bit of bleeding with my last pregnancy, so I wasn't too concerned, but we called the doctor just to be safe. Off we went to have a scan, just to check everything was OK. And, before the scan technician said anything, I knew straight away when I saw the screen. My heart wanted a different result, but I knew that we had lost the baby.

In all the other scans we had seen – both in this pregnancy and the last – the little thing had always showed so much joyous movement. It was like it was already so happy to be joining the world and our family. But this one was different. It was lifeless. No movement. No joy. No heartbeat.

My own heart broke in that moment, and stayed broken for a long time. How could I have become so attached to something so quickly that I felt so devastated when it was taken away? I had only had such a short time connecting to it. But it fucking hurt.

I can't really find the reason why this happened. I've searched for one.

But it just happened.

Why does any loss happen, I guess? For anyone? Maybe we're not always meant to know why. Maybe not everything is meant to be explainable.

I think I did have faith somewhere inside me that there was likely to have been a bigger plan. Bigger than me. Bigger than us. And whether or not it was true, at the very least that faith helped ease the pain just a little. So I chose to hold on to it.

I won't always know why.

Losing our baby was the start of what would become an unhealthy, distorted relationship with my body that would last for quite a few years. I became angry at her. My body. She had failed me. She had failed our baby. She had failed our whole family.

And I blamed her. I resented her for not keeping our baby alive. I felt like I had done all the right things in my head and in my heart, but my body had just let me down. She had let us all down.

So, somewhere in my pain-filled logic, I subconsciously decided that my body should be punished. She should immediately mould into the perfect form so she might hopefully one day house another baby properly.

I joined a gym. Yes. A gym. Extreme measures, I know. I wasn't exactly the gym-going type. But putting my energy into getting perfectly fit seemed a lot easier than feeling the loss. And what's the downside of getting physically healthy, right?

But there was no healthy incentive behind my motivation. There was only grief, distraction and sadness.

I slowly became obsessed. Obsessed with making my disappointing body perfect. Pushing her to the extreme to make sure she would never fail me again. My focus was unwavering. My determination strict. My target non-negotiable. I went from mostly feeling so light, comfortable and happy in my own skin to treating my body like she was a constantly underachieving employee who I had to harshly discipline to get a job done right.

I became so plugged into my detrimental goal that I barely noticed that I was simultaneously unplugging from my relationship with my partner, and from many other parts of my life. I was letting my fear of ever going through this again lead the way. My partner and I slowly drifted apart, and before long we had ended our relationship.

My relationship with my body, however, carried on heading south. Right before my eyes, it was distorting but I didn't even notice. I didn't want to. I just wanted to live in denial for a while.

Ahhhhhh, the luxury of hindsight, hey?

It's basically like having a TV screen of your own life playing back while you watch and count how many times you wish you had said to yourself, 'Just don't be a dickhead.'

My body is not to blame. She is always doing her best.

Life is sometimes just not fair. Accepting that makes some things easier.

For most of my career I've felt deeply connected to whatever album I've been making at the time. Even years after writing, recording and releasing my songs, I can still connect to them and feel the same emotion and genuine bond I felt when first writing or recording them.

As an album, *The Captain* has an innocence and naivety that I genuinely felt at the time and naturally put into it, so I still feel the same things when I hear or play all those songs now.

Barricades & Brickwalls has both a strong and a vulnerable voice throughout – a voice that I was only just discovering within myself. So there's still a real sense of the emotions connected to all the songs on that album, too.

Wayward Angel was the first album I made after becoming a mother.

I was getting to know a whole new side of myself, experiencing things I'd never done before, so there's an excitement and an imagination on that record that I was swept up in – and still feel now when I hear it or play it.

This sense of connection works both ways. If it's there, and I'm connected to myself and my creativity, I will usually stay connected to it no matter how many years have passed between me making a song and listening to it or playing it again. But if I'm disconnected from myself and my creativity, then I can't really expect to feel much more from it than exactly that: disconnect.

I've never really felt obligated to make music that pleases everybody, or even music that will please future me. I don't really think that far ahead. It's mostly just been about how I felt in a moment. Who I was at that point in my life.

• • •

In 2005, I wanted to make album number four. Music life had settled into a bit more of a rhythm since my last album, but things had been a little up and down as well, I guess. Losing the baby, dealing with a break-up, finding a new love and wrangling a three-year-old every day. Another new normal.

Life was OK.

But, to be honest, the thought of really connecting to myself on any kind of deep, vulnerable level again in order to make another album seemed fucking exhausting and a bit inconvenient. So this time, I decided to try a new creative approach.

My inner foghorn hadn't really been around in a while. Living up at the surface was much easier, less emotional, and I always got a lot more day-to-day shit done. So it was time to just start writing from that surface level. No heart, no soul, no depth, no painstaking therapy session put into a lyric. Just good, clean, scheduled songwriting.

I came up with a plan. I put a couple of months aside to write this new album, worked on it every day, clocking on at 9 am and knocking off at 5 pm. I churned out a bunch of surface-inspired songs, and that gave my heart and sleeve a little rest for a bit. And I made a record called *Carnival.*

I don't mind that record. It's nice ... enough. But I do not feel connected to it at all. I never feel a desire to hear the songs or play them. I never feel any emotion connected to them. I never think about them. And no one ever requests any song off that whole record.

Now, I get requests for songs from every other album I've ever made. Some more than others, of course, but every album gets a little bit of love and attention from different people from all different walks of life all over the place. Every album except *Carnival.*

I don't hate it, and I'm not embarrassed by it. I don't feel negative feelings for it. It's that I just don't have any feelings for it full stop.

It just exists.

I don't see that album as a waste of time. Instead, it feels a lot more like a lesson that I taught to myself. Or maybe a bit more like a masterclass.

If I don't feel connected to myself and my creativity, then I won't feel connected to my songs and albums while I am making them – and I will never really feel connected to them at all. If I don't feel connected to them, then it's highly likely that not many other people will, either.

• • •

The comment people have most frequently made to me over the years is, 'I don't really like country music, but I like your music.'

I used to be a bit confused by this. *How can they like my music if they don't like country music?* I'd think. *I'm a country singer and I write country songs.*

But I still always took it as a compliment.

Now, having learnt more about creativity and connection, I think that, when we really love someone else's creative work, what we are probably loving more than anything else is their 'connection' with the work. It might actually have nothing to do with a genre.

Maybe we are linking up with that person's truth, their heart, their passion, their intention – rather than just the song we are hearing at the time.

We are probably connecting to the authenticity that they put into the song more than we are to a particular style.

So I think that the more of my true self I put into my work, the more others can probably feel it too. And I find this is true not just in music. I feel it in so many other creative things too. I remember when I saw a David Bromley painting for the first time, I felt so many emotions. Passion. Heart. Intensity. Love. Recklessness. Now, I don't know a thing about art at all and I've never really been into it – most of the time, I can't tell the difference between what most people would probably call high-end art and what my kids paint at home in their bedrooms – so I didn't have a clue about who Bromley was or his work. But when I first saw that painting, I got completely lost in it. Just staring at it while something stirred inside me. I wasn't even sure what it was or what it meant, but it swept me up. I weirdly felt like I knew a part of the artist just by looking at his painting. Like I could feel what he felt when he created it.

But maybe it wasn't so much about him or the painting.

Maybe I was feeling the authentic connection *between* him and his painting. The creative link. The vulnerability that he so bravely let take over when he created that artwork.

I didn't quite understand it. But maybe I didn't really need to? Maybe that's the beauty of creativity? Not always understanding it in your head. Instead, just feeling it in your heart and soul.

When I see an old piece of carved furniture and I have no idea of the story behind it, I can still feel something special in the room. I am drawn to it for some reason, and it's about more than what I see. There's a history in it. An energy that someone felt and held around it when it was created. Something authentic given to it. Something that is impossible to feel from a factory-made piece of furniture. Instead of being flawless, finished and polished, that piece of furniture is full of heart, emotion and imperfection.

These are the sorts of things that I love to surround myself with now. Things that I feel the connection in.

And I truly hope that, when people hear my music, at the very least they feel something. Even if they don't like it. Maybe my authentic connection to my creativity is enough to just stir something. Yeah, I know sometimes that 'stirring something' causes some people to block their ears, but it's still better than nothing at all I reckon.

The more connected I am to *who* I am, the more of my authentic self I can put into my work. And the more I connect to my work, the more other people can too. Communicating through creativity is my definition of my 'job'. And what a beautiful job it is. I get paid to connect to my authentic self.

Authenticity is the easiest sell.

Not everything will turn out exactly how you plan.

9.

There's a difference between being a 'giver' and being a 'people pleaser'

Around the time I made *Wayward Angel*, I also got married. We'd put some money aside, but a big, fancy wedding wasn't really my style. So, when the time came to start planning, both Shane and I decided that the money would probably be better used somewhere else.

On a charity visit a while earlier, I had met a little boy at Ronald McDonald House who'd stolen my heart. He had leukaemia, and I noticed him straight away in the crowd of kids because of his Spider-Man T-shirt. My son Talon loved Spider-Man – the superhero was all he ever talked about (still is now, at age twenty-two). Little Jai was

Above: Two-year-old me with my older brother, Nash.

Right: Me and my mum, Diane.

Below: Me on my third birthday with my dad, Bill.

Above: Dad and I on the cover of a local calendar. Everyone thought it was father and son.

Left: My cousins, uncle, Nash and I washing our hair in cattle troughs.

Above: My wild pet rabbit Jackson, named after Jackson Browne.

Left: Me on the Nullarbor.

Above: Worm and me.

Right: Me and Worm with our *Seinfeld* shrine.

Left: Mum, Brady Blade and me on the Emmylou Harris tour in 2001.

Below: Nash, Cori, me, Mum and Worm.

Above: Me with my first proper guitar, DeGruchy.

Right: Talon, me and Arlo.

Above: Arlo and Buddy.

Left: Warren Williams, Poet, me and baby Barkley.

Above: My current touring band and crew. The best of eggs.

Below: Poet, Brando, me, Talon and Arlo.

about the same age as Talon, and I got to know his blended family a bit while we were there. When I told Shane all about them and the ongoing medical bills and their financial struggles, we knew we'd rather give them the money than have a proper wedding. We still get updates from Jai and his family to this day. We're always happy to learn how well he's doing.

Instead of a wedding, we had a small BBQ in our backyard. I wore a Bob Dylan tour shirt and blue jeans with bare feet. Worm stood next to me as my 'mate of honour', with a stubby in one hand and a smoke in the other.

It's always felt very natural for me to give. I'm sure my mum's influence early on had a lot to do with that. It's something that I always get a lot of pure joy from. But, as much as I hate to admit this, for a while, the lines around being a 'giver' would blur a lot for me, and I would end up losing sight of why I gave.

If I'm brutally honest with myself – which is making me cringe a bit as I write – I can now look back on many times in my life when my intention around giving hasn't always been quite as honourable and pure as I've convinced myself it was.

Sometimes, my intentions for being a 'giver' would be quite different from what I was truly willing to see. Sometimes I was giving just from wanting to please people. Sometimes from not being able to say no. Sometimes from wanting the credit and attention. Sometimes from wanting to distract myself from other things. Sometimes from wanting to feel needed. And sometimes just out of habit alone.

Now, it feels pretty damn uncomfortable to admit all of that … but a long way down the track I would start to figure out that being honest with myself about shit like this is the only way for me to actually start to live as the person I wanna be. The person I know I truly am. Living my inner foghorn on the outside too.

I can't just give myself the title of being a 'giver' when my intentions around giving are in all the wrong places. That's not so much 'being a giver' as it is 'being a dickhead'. And that's not who I want to be.

Eventually, I would end up having some more honest conversations with myself about my true intentions, and that helped me to start giving from the right places again. Giving from my actual heart.

• • •

I was also about to learn the hard way that, if I am busy being a 'giver' but don't take the time to fill my own cup, I'll have nowhere to draw from. And if my cup is always broken, then it's gonna drain very quickly.

Once again, I had a number one record on the ARIA charts. I was in the middle of a sell-out album tour of Australia. I was newly married. I'd just bought a brand-new house. I had supportive friends. I had a beautiful family. I had a thriving career. I had everything that anyone could ever want.

But, somewhere along the way, I had disconnected from myself. I had tuned out my inner foghorn, covered her up and packed her away under the shell of a woman that I had become. Because, somewhere underneath the perfect life on paper and all the accolades, I was fading away. Emotionally and physically.

But I told myself daily that everything was fine. Not just fine. Everything was great! What could I ever possibly have to complain about? What could I ever possibly have to feel sad about?

My life was perfect. In theory.

I just had to keep pedalling. Pedalling as fast as I could on my little bike of life. The wheels had to keep turning at all times.

Balancing, steering and riding along, all at the same time, I crammed that little basket on the front of my life bike with all my albums, my tours, my successes, my son, my husband, my family, my band mates, my friends, my home life, my work colleagues, my expectations, my opportunities, my creativity, my finances, my record label, my publishers, my fans and my happiness. Every now and then, a normal human emotion would pop up to the surface – sadness or frustration or weakness or exhaustion or overwhelmedness (is that even a word?) – but I would push it aside. I had no room in my little bike basket for anything else.

And, anyway, I didn't really even have a right to feel any negative emotions. I was so lucky to have all this happening to me. An incredible dream career, the gift of motherhood, a loving family, adoring fans … I would have to be the biggest ungrateful idiot to feel anything negative right now. And of course, if I ever did let myself feel anything negative, it was matched with a feeling of guilt.

So it was best for me to just feel good all the time. I managed to convince myself somewhere along the line that there was just no room for negative emotions at all. I should only feel positive ones and just plough through.

On the surface I had total control of that bike, but somewhere underneath my life felt full of pressure and expectation, and completely out of my control. I had so many people and big companies counting on me. Family members, record label, management, fans, friends, band mates – all relying on me to stay on that bike, keep pedalling and just get shit done.

I had slowly been giving away my control to everyone else. But the ironic thing was, I don't even think they were really asking for it. Sure, they would take it if I willingly gave it away, but I'm not really sure anyone was ever putting as much pressure on me as I was putting on myself. I could have said no if I'd wanted to. I wasn't in some kind of music mafia! They weren't going to have me knee-capped if I refused to do the after-gig signing or the record-store appearance.

At what point had I convinced myself that I didn't have a choice? At what point had I convinced myself that I couldn't say no? At what point had I convinced myself that I didn't have my own voice anymore?

I was becoming a people pleaser. I was letting the outer voices become louder than my inner foghorn.

And the funny thing about becoming a people pleaser? It pleases people. Yep. But only for a while. Once I started losing myself and became disconnected from my inner foghorn, I started disconnecting from other people as well. People who meant a lot to me. I was pleasing them on one level but creating division on another.

There I was, people-pleasing, covering up my true feelings, completely tuned out of my inner foghorn, disconnecting from myself and everyone, abandoning myself ... and living the fucking dream.

Deal with shit when it comes up or it'll come back to bite you in the arse.

Still living with my underlying unhealthy view of my own body, there was one thing I was controlling in my life: every single little bit of food I put in my mouth, every calorie I consumed, every number on the scale every day, and how I looked in my mirror. I was losing weight. Fast. And I kinda liked that feeling. Or did I?

On one hand, I liked the feeling of being fully in control of something for a change, and I liked the feeling of being thin like the beautiful girls on the covers of magazines, but then I would look in the mirror and I didn't look like me anymore. I looked too thin. I looked unwell. I couldn't see my spark or my free spirit. So I just stopped looking in the mirror. I liked the number on the scale much more.

I took note of every single calorie that went into my body, including the toothpaste I may have swallowed while brushing my teeth. I starved myself for days, then binged on food because I was so hungry – but every bit of food that went into my body felt like poison in my stomach, eating away at my insides, and I would just vomit it all back up.

I'm embarrassed to say that I really didn't even consider the fact that I might have had some kind of serious problem. I mean, in my mind, it was really only teenage girls with body-image problems who suffered from eating disorders. That wasn't me. I was a thirty-year-old role model for girls to look up to.

My friend Bern, Worm's wife, would try to open up honest conversations with me about my obvious problem. She tried to help, to get me to see that something was wrong (real friends unfortunately – or fortunately – tell us what we don't want to hear sometimes) but I would brush it off. I stayed in denial.

It took quite a few of those conversations and an emotional collapse from exhaustion to get me to see what I had been fighting against seeing. Then one day, I finally admitted to myself, and to a few of those people close to me, that I had an eating disorder. In that moment, I felt everything. All the sadness, all the frustration, all the exhaustion, all the weakness, all the overwhelming worries, all the insecurities, all the unease, all the uncertainty … all the pressure and all the fear.

But underneath all of it was my little inner foghorn. She was rising up and giving me one strong feeling that actually over-rode all of it. I felt something I hadn't felt in a long time: relief.

I surrendered.

My little inner foghorn was no longer silenced. With the help of my friends and family, I'd given her voice back.

Through months and months of therapy and some inner work to learn some obvious but hard things about myself, I started to see one of the most important lessons – that life doesn't work very well without feeling all the stuff at some stage. Good and bad.

It's unrealistic to stay in a bubble seeing only the good shit and ignoring the rest.

But, as opposed to feeding negative emotions just for the sake of it, I needed to learn how to acknowledge those negative feelings, how to work with them to get to the bottom of where they came from.

It's a fine line to walk, I know, but ignoring those real emotions – even if I don't like them or want them – will only cause them to find other, distorted ways to surface.

I can't just keep pedalling non-stop forever.

Sometimes I need to empty that basket and take that little bike in for a few repairs.

Breathe.

A few years back, one of my favourite musicians, John Butler, asked me to be a part of an important cause very close to his heart. He and his wife, Danielle, are beautiful friends of mine, and I respect them dearly and would generally drop anything to help them out – but the request came at a time when, both physically and emotionally, I was dealing with some things that were quite a struggle. I knew that my mind, heart and body needed some healing, rest and time to reboot … but I really didn't want to say no to John.

I just thought, *Well, I have to say yes.*

John is such a beautiful musician and human, always doing such good things for our industry and for the world. How could I possibly say no to his request?

Then my little inner foghorn popped up. 'Now, come on, Kase,' she said. 'Your cup is broken and is draining fast. You need some time to repair and fill it back up before you start drawing from it to give to others again.'

She was right.

So I begrudgingly figured it might have to be a 'no' this time. I started thinking of excuses that would be valid enough that John wouldn't think I was being insensitive. I didn't want to feel guilty for saying no to such an important cause and good friend. Maybe I could say I was sick and couldn't make it? Maybe I could say I was booked up that week? John didn't know my health status or exact schedule …

But my inner foghorn popped up again. This time she was a little more to the point. 'Kase, just tell him the truth,' she said. 'Firstly, it's not your job to worry about how someone else will react if you just bring your true self and honesty to the line. And secondly, don't be a dickhead. Do you actually think you're so fucking important that John Butler won't be able to handle hearing "no" from you? Pull your head in, Chambo.'

So I told John the truth. That I was going through a really tough

time and had no emotional strength to be able to properly give much to anyone else right now.

I sat looking at the phone and waited for the response with bated breath and tense anxiety that I pretended I wasn't feeling.

The long-awaited, dreaded text message came through. But, instead of giving me a lecture about how I obviously didn't care much about this very important cause, John lovingly said to me that he totally understood, and respected my honesty, vulnerability and decision to look after myself first. He then offered his shoulder to lean on any time I needed it, reminding me that I was not ever alone.

Real friends respect an honest answer.

He also added, as he often does, 'Keep being brave for all the things that matter most.'

Saying no doesn't make me a dickhead.

It's hard to draw from a broken cup.

'BROKEN CUP'

Learning to say no has been a roller-coaster ride for me over the years. Sometimes I've done it easily and naturally, sometimes I've had to remind myself to do it, and sometimes I've flat out refused to do it even when I know I should.

It can be hard to survive in the music industry and stay true to yourself at the same time, but I really believe that finding a way to make some peace with saying no (and doing it without being a dickhead) is the only way for me to find some kind of balance. It's unrealistic to please everyone, anyway. I know that turning down the outer noise and tuning back in to my inner foghorn is what works best.

It's certainly taken a bit to get used to saying no, though. I actually may never get completely used to it, but I remind myself all the time when I'm faced with things to honestly ask myself why I am saying yes or no.

Am I saying yes to fill my heart and soul?

Am I saying yes because my inner foghorn is giving me the thumbs up?

Am I saying yes to fulfil a future purpose that means something to me?

Am I saying yes from a place of love and compassion?

Or ... am I just saying yes because it makes me feel uncomfortable to say no? Because society tells me I should?

Am I just saying yes out of habit, and not really thinking about whether it truly matches up with me?

Am I just saying yes to fill my own ego?

And, on the flip side, am I saying no because it genuinely doesn't resonate with me? Am I saying no because my inner foghorn is guiding me wisely towards that? Because it doesn't match up with my future purpose? Because my cup is broken and draining too quickly?

Or ... am I just saying no out of fear of failure? Out of fear of rejection? Out of fear of disappointing someone, even though it doesn't resonate with me?

Am I saying no because I'm just being an arsehole?

It won't always be a straight-out answer, but it's still always mine to decide. It's up to me to be honest with myself about my decision.

Living in a world that often feels controlled and restrained has shown me that, the more I create my own boundaries based on my own reasons, the more freedom I really do have.

Unlearning old things is just as important as learning new ones.

What better way to slow down an out-of-control and busy public life than with an under-the-radar, unadvertised little gig to a small crowd every Thursday night at a pub down the road from my house? It certainly gave my husband and me a bit more grounding and some time to catch our breath. But giving too much time to newlyweds also meant another baby was soon on the way.

During our downtime, Shane and I had been writing a record together called *Rattlin' Bones* that we would later go on to record at Jimmy Barnes's house, which has nothing to do with the story – I just like name-dropping Jimmy Barnes whenever I can. It was released through Liberation Music and marked the beginning of a beautiful relationship with Warren Costello, Michael Gudinski, Frank Stivala and Mushroom Group Australia. All of this played a big part in bringing back my love for and connection to music.

But, to begin with, every Thursday night was just about The Lost

Dogs. Our little low-key band with my dad and some mates jamming along just for fun. We played our favourite covers every week for nine months while I happily grew our child. I loved the gig, of course, but by the time I was ten days overdue, I was really hoping to miss the next jam altogether – instead, I hoped Shane and I would be meeting our long-awaited child.

When Thursday rolled around, I had started having some mild labour pains and was due for a check-up with my obstetrician, so we headed straight up to the hospital, ready to finally get this show on the road. But I was only two centimetres dilated, so I was sent home with strict orders to rest up and wait until I was further along in labour.

I decided that my time in early labour would be better spent – and I'd be distracted – if I was doing a gig. Off we went to the pub. I set up my guitar, graced the stage (not very gracefully) and informed our regular audience that any requests for songs with extreme high notes that night could result in a messy occurrence.

There was certainly a slightly nervous energy to the gig's vibe – and especially from Shane – but we made it through singing country songs while in early labour.

Our baby, Arlo, didn't end up joining the world until well into the next day. Time well spent.

Don't waste time just dilating away.

It's not my job to please everyone. Or anyone.

10.

Lead with an open heart

I had just finished breastfeeding my son when there was a knock at the door. It was the electrician I'd called earlier, so I let him in, showed him to our power box, offered him a drink and chatted for a bit about the unseasonably cool weather we'd had lately.

He quickly fixed the problem, packed up his things, warmly thanked me for my business, then hurried off out the door to his next job.

As I shut the door behind him, I looked down. My bare, leaking boob had been out – and exposed – the whole time.

Fuck.

I guess I had a choice.

Do I choose to die of embarrassment like Elaine in the *Seinfeld* episode when she accidentally sent a Christmas card with a photo of her – and her nipple on full display – to all her family, work colleagues and friends?

Or do I choose to just laugh at myself?

I thought of Jerry's take on it: it's just a nipple. We've all got 'em. No big deal.

Yeah. It's just a boob. (And it was my good one.)

We can choose how we see things.

I spent some time in prison in 2009. OK, it was only a visit for a few days, and I went as a songwriter, but it still changed my life.

I went as part of the ABC series *Jailbirds* in which the wonderful choral instructor and opera singer Jonathon Welch created a choir with the women who were inmates at Tarrengower Prison in Victoria. I'd been asked to spend a few days with the women, to help them write an original song as part of this rehabilitative project. I was already in writing mode – I was at work on my sixth album, *Little Bird* – and I thought this co-writing project would be an interesting opportunity for me to teach some of my writing skills to others. Little did I know that I'd end up learning way more from these women than the other way around.

I had never been to a prison before. When I first arrived, the show's production team and I shared the obvious pleasantries and awkward introductions, then I was given a general overview of the next few days, and my guitar case was thoroughly searched for weapons and contraband. Not your average gig proceeding.

Inside the prison, Jonathon and I sat down in a circle with the women, overseen by prison guards, and the two of us bantered back and forth, sharing some song ideas and working a little on the chorus I'd come up with beforehand. The women were hesitant to contribute much – they stayed mostly quiet and withdrawn, self-conscious about being in this foreign creative-writing environment. This was understandable. None of them were really musical in a professional sense in any way, none of them had ever written any kind of lyric or poem before, and not many of them had ever thought about singing before this choir project.

That's OK, I told myself. *Tomorrow is going to be more about writing the song anyway, so I can easily lead that to where it needs to go then. Today is just about breaking the ice. For all of us.*

Outside of their usual strict schedules, these women only had a little bit of time dedicated to filming this out-of-the-ordinary project each day. So the cameras were soon turned off, and I put the guitar away. Some of the women came up to get my autograph, and uncomfortably showed their appreciation for my visit. My sister-in-law Veronica had come with me and, now that the cameras were off, she was happy to come and join in. Together, we took the opportunity to find out a little more about all these women.

I had been told beforehand that, while it was OK for me to interact and chat freely with the prisoners, I was not to ask what they were in for – especially not while the cameras were rolling. But, in the back of my mind, I was genuinely intrigued about what kind of backstory ended someone up in a place like this. What made them 'different' from me? Veronica and I started asking a few 'normal' questions – things like, 'Where are you from? Do you have children? What are your interests?'

Slowly, the women came around. They started talking. With every question, they would open up a little bit more, and then they started to share their lives *before* prison. With every bit of interest we showed in who they were outside of these walls, their faces lit up and they took their own walls down. As each woman spoke, the other inmates would gather around her and chime in, telling us about her hidden talents like proud mothers. 'Oh, you should hear Heather sing! She has a beautiful voice.'

They talked about their hometowns, their families, their jobs, their careers, their relationships, their hobbies, their fears, their mistakes, their addictions, their triumphs, their faults, their faith, their misjudgements, their upbringings, their passions, their goals, their hopes, their plans and their dreams. There was *no* difference between us. No difference at all. These were real women with real lives. Real feelings. Real choices. Real circumstances. Making the kinds of real fuck-ups any of us are capable of making.

And when they questioned me about my life, I shared my fears, mistakes and downfalls.

All of our hearts were open and honest. And together.

Veronica and I left the prison for the night, and went to stay in our comfortable hotel room down the road, which we outwardly noted with gratitude we were able to leave freely, whenever we wanted. In that room, we reflected on the day. It had opened both our eyes more than we'd expected.

• • •

The next morning at the prison, we were welcomed by a very different energy in the room from our first moments together the morning before. The connection we'd made during our off-camera interactions opening up to each other had withstood the night, and it felt like walking into a room full of old friends. All the women were smiling and eager. With their hearts on their sleeves, they were open and ready to share what creativity they had inside them, to show the strong voices that they had let become so silenced and had been hidden for so many years.

The feeling in the room was beautiful and supportive. One of the women announced to me, 'Sal wrote a verse to the song overnight!' Then, as Sal shared the verse with the whole group, they applauded and praised her heartfelt, honest contribution – and then, together, we all added to it.

When the group sang together, what had seemed like a half-hearted and timid sound the day before turned into a fully blown powerful choir. Those voices were so strong my heart felt like it was going to burst.

This was women supporting women in the truest sense. Women digging deep, against all odds, to tune into their inner foghorns and give themselves – and each other – a voice again. A voice they had lost, or been told throughout their lives they didn't even have. A voice they were brave enough to use to communicate their deepest, darkest feelings in front of all these other people.

These women weren't professional singers. Far from it. They hadn't necessarily even been around music in their lives. They didn't have musical families, and hadn't grown up on stage like I had. They were so far outside their comfort zones. But they were doing it! Digging deep and opening up, and it was the bravest thing I had ever seen. Even the prison guards ended up singing along.

Across the room, through our tears, Veronica and I shared a look. We knew we were lucky to be there, in the presence of ordinary women doing extraordinary things for themselves and for one another. Letting their inner foghorns rise up.

Over those short few days, I realised more than ever what a powerful difference a woman can make for another woman, simply by giving her a chance to feel seen and heard.

There's no sound more beautiful than a jailbird's voice set free.

One afternoon when Talon was nine and Arlo was four, I asked them to clean their room. They shared a room at this point, and had let it get into a disgusting state, as boys' rooms generally do. Clothes, toys, food, dishes, wet towels lying around on the floor.

I had just asked them for the *third* time to clean it and been ignored once again because they were both way too invested in the new and exciting fighting positions they were posing their Power Rangers toys in to listen to me.

I had seriously had enough.

I worked hard keeping this house clean! I kept food on the table. I kept clothes on their backs. The very least that they could do to contribute to this family was to tidy their room when they were asked. I was going to let them know straight out how disrespectful and disobedient they were being, and it was time to make sure they heard it.

So I stormed into the room, stood at the door on my overworked-mother high horse and started yelling:

'I HAVE TOLD YOU THREE TIMES TO CLEAN THIS

DAMN ROOM, AND YOU HAVE IGNORED ME OVER AND OVER AGAIN! I AM SICK OF IT. NOW, GET UP THIS SECOND AND I WANT TO SEE THIS ROOM SPOTLESS BY THE TIME I –'

But instead of finishing my significant rant with words, I released with the same force I had tried to put into my demands a giant, unmistakable, loud fart.

The boys went from startled fear to hysterical laughter, and in that instant I lost any authority I had ever had as a parent. There was no coming back. There was nothing I could do or say to regain any control or power as a respected guardian.

My third child was yet to arrive – my daughter, Poet – and that might have given me the chance to try to redeem myself as a parent.

But, obviously, once Poet was old enough the boys told her the story of what happens when Mum gets cross and starts yelling.

To this day, if I get to the point where I've had enough and raise my voice even a little bit, my kids will say, 'Ooooh, Mum's getting angry … Let her go and she might let one rip!'

I know there's so many other reasons that I shouldn't yell at my kids (psychological damage, blah, blah, blah) but, if I'm truly honest, the main thing that really stops me from doing it again is the lingering embarrassment of the infamous exploding fart.

Yelling at my kids can be extremely damaging.

Since Talon's dad and I had separated when Talon was two years old, he'd been going back and forth between our houses for a long time. Aside from the initial break-up bullshit we all go through, Cori and I ended up remaining great friends and he is still part of my immediate tribe to this day.

Talon happily drifted between his two homes like all was as it should be. When he was a little kid, he and I had even written a song together called 'Two Houses' after he'd said to me, 'Mum, it's sad. Some of my friends at school only have one house because their mum and dad still live together. I have two houses. Lucky me.'

Anyway, one day when Talon was about ten, Cori and I were chatting together and started wondering if either of us had ever had a proper conversation with our son about religion. We were pretty sure neither of us had spent half as much time talking to him about that

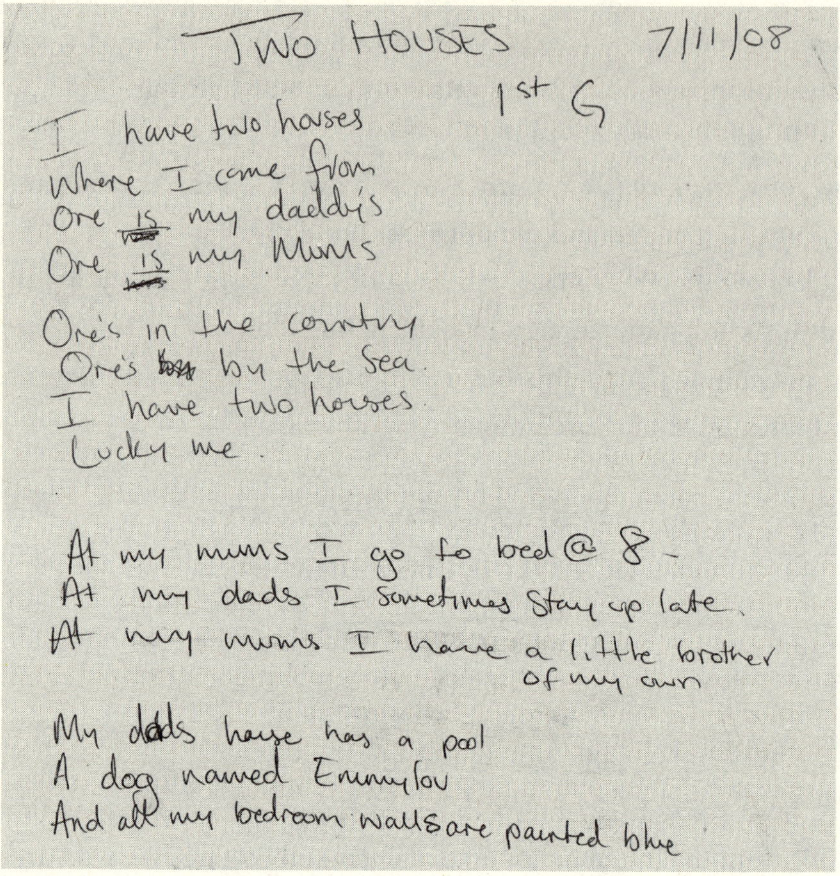

TWO HOUSES 7/11/08

1st G

I have two houses
Where I come from
One is my daddy's
One is my Mums

One's in the country
One's by the sea.
I have two houses
Lucky me.

At my mums I go to bed @ 8 –
At my dads I sometimes stay up late.
At my mums I have a little brother
of my own

My dads house has a pool
A dog named Emmylou
And all my bedroom walls are painted blue

as we had about which Aussie Rules football team he should follow. (Cori won that one with the West Coast Eagles.)

Outside of my early upbringing, of course, I wasn't really religious at all in a traditional sense – but I guess I had a lot of spiritual beliefs that I lived by, we played a lot of gospel music at my home, and I often used references to God and the Bible in my songs. Talon was always exposed to all of that. Meanwhile, his dad was a staunch atheist at this point. Thinking about that, we realised we might be well overdue a conversation with Talon to help curb some of the confusion that was likely going on in his little mind.

So, we set some time aside together, as co-parents, to sit him down with open hearts and have a talk with him. We were ready to help his growing mind somehow grasp one of humanity's hardest and most complicated topics.

'Tal,' I started, 'are you getting a bit confused, mate, going between Dad's house and my house, about whether you believe in God or not?'

'No,' he replied matter-of-factly. 'I'm not confused at all. When I'm at your place I believe in God, and when I'm at Dad's I don't.'

Then he happily got up and left.

Let people believe in their own way.

Just after Poet's birth, my brother and his wife booked me to host and perform at the Foggy Mountain jam festival, which they ran each year for their local community in the lower Hunter Valley region, in New South Wales. It was a beautiful little festival to be a part of, so I was happy to oblige.

With the festival about to begin, the day was running smoothly so far. I'd gathered all the information I had to deliver as part of my hosting duties, and I was all set to sing harmonies for other artists, to help with full band change-overs and to give my own performances … until I remembered another responsibility I'd taken on. That of being a breastfeeding mother to my newborn baby daughter. I'd forgotten to organise any other way for this kid to get fed while I was working on stage for the next five hours.

By the time I realised this, it was too late to express milk, I had no formula sorted and I didn't want the festival to run late. So with my free spirit leading the way, I said 'fuck it' and just breastfed my baby on stage throughout the day while introducing artists, pointing the way to the festival toilets (not with my nipple) and singing sad country songs to over 500 strangers.

Meh. It's not like a total stranger hadn't seen my boobs before. Or at least one of them anyway.

Needless to say, Poet does not really like to be reminded of her first on-stage appearance.

The more I let go of judgement and let my free spirit fly, the more shit I get done.

For the most part, my job out on the road, travelling all around Australia as a touring singer/songwriter, had brought a lot of beautiful experiences into my children's lives. But everything has another side, of course. Travelling around with me has also often meant that sometimes we've had to miss out on things back at home – things like school functions, presentation days and parent–teacher meetings. OK, I'll be honest. Some of these things I've been quietly happy to miss out on, cos they sounded fucking boring. But often there were things I did wish we could have been there for.

Over the years, I've definitely found it hard at times to keep up with trying to be a 'good mum'. Juggling the logistics of balancing a career and a tour. Trying to do my best parenting while also releasing another album with my husband that was aptly named *Wreck & Ruin* as it would eventually lead to a divorce in there somewhere. It all definitely added some extra complications for a while.

I also started discovering that how you approach parenting can actually be quite different from one child to the next. As parents, we (or is it just me?) often put a lot of attention and energy into encouraging our firstborn to participate in and join every extra-curricular activity and opportunity presented. Then we attend, document and proudly display every moment. But we put in a little less effort when it comes to documenting, displaying and drawing on parenting morals for the second-born kid. Maybe only one or two awards make the fridge, and a certificate awarded to Arlo Nicholson for 'Trying to concentrate and do his best work' (he actually got that award once) doesn't quite make the cut. By kid number three? Well, she is eating four-day-old Vegemite sandwiches from under the couch and I am telling her that dance class was cancelled due to an infestation of radioactive spiders when the truth is it's because I

Certificate of Achievement

Awarded to

Arlo Nicholson KB.

For

Trying to concentrate and do his best work.

Date 22nd March 2013 · Class Teacher

Principal

COPACABANA PUBLIC SCHOOL

EFFORT EARNS SUCCESS

LOLA TERRIFIC

PRINCIPAL'S AWARD

just can't be fucked taking her.

I'm extremely grateful for the help I've had over the years. My kids' fathers have taken their fair share of the load, and my mum and other family members and friends have always been there to help out. The public schools that all my kids have gone to have been extremely supportive of our travels, and I'm also fortunate to have a flexible job where I kinda get to work for myself. But being a working mum in any capacity can be tricky. Even based on just perception alone.

As a mother, you're expected to do everything, remember everything, get everything right, juggle a million things at once, look presentable, say the right things, prevent things before they happen, fix things after they happen, be good at everything you try, make sure your kids are clean and perfect, always be on time and not lose your shit while doing it all. And if you don't fulfil this working-mum brief, you can be sure a certain amount of guilt is going to creep in – just enough to motivate you to get straight back on that hamster wheel and keep running.

I was at home one day, attempting a half-hearted job of cleaning Arlo and Talon's bedroom (I wasn't going to yell at them to do it again, of course) while they were at school. Talon was at high school, Arlo in primary, and Poet was annoyingly following me around at home. Then I found an old school note under Arlo's bed. One I hadn't seen before.

BOOK WEEK COSTUME PARADE.

The date? Tomorrow.

Fuck.

Guilt. Guilt. *I'm a shit mother. I should have been on top of this.*

OK, maybe he can wear one of the old costumes that I made for Talon from another year …

I'd certainly put a lot more effort into my firstborn's Book Week costumes. And, as if it wasn't bad enough to be standing there clutching at the hope that the other parents wouldn't notice the corners I was cutting by recycling a costume from another year and another child, my guilt took it up a notch. 'Not only have you not given Arlo the Book Week costume effort that he deserves,' it said, 'but remember he also actually *missed* last year's Book Week parade altogether because you were off travelling for your precious career …' My poor second child, now the quintessential Middle Child.

'OK, Kase,' I said to myself. 'This is it. This is your one moment to make up for every mothering mistake you've ever made in your entire life. Dig deep. You've got this. It all hinges on this one costume. This costume will define your nurturing competence and prove to you and to all the other school mothers that you deserve the treasured gift you've been given that is your child.'

And deep I dug!

I cut, I glued, I sewed, I painted with every part of my being for hours and hours until that giant red Angry Birds papier-mâché head was finished and perfect.

I stood back, exhausted and proud, to admire my exemplary parenting talents as evidenced by my crafting skills and attention to detail.

Then my phone rang.

'Hi, Kasey, this is Mrs Woodham from the primary school. I think you've forgotten to pick Arlo up from school. He's been waiting outside on the street by himself for forty-five minutes.'

If I had stopped worrying about what kind of mother I was 'supposed' to be – according to the pressures of the school-mum society, which I had partly made up in my own head anyway – I might have actually been there when my kid needed me.

I rushed to the school, and when I picked him up I said, 'Arlo, I am so sorry I was late, mate. But I made you the best Angry Birds costume for the Book Week parade tomorrow.'

'Thanks, Mum,' he replied, 'but my friend Blake and I are gonna go as pirates.'

I am a good mum.
Except for when I'm not.

'ARLO'

In between babies, albums and giant papier-mâché heads, I would always get back to touring.

One night after playing a gig in the Rio Theatre in Santa Cruz, California, I was sitting on my tour bus in my pyjamas, getting ready to turn in for the night, when my dad came onto the bus.

'There's a guy here with his wife who would really like to meet you,' he said. 'Can I bring them in to say hi? They are lovely people and really big fans of yours. I think he said he's an apple farmer or something. Granny Smith apples are my favourite. Hope he has some of them with him.'

'Yeah, no worries,' I said.

So Steve and Janet came onto the bus, and we all hung out for a while like we were old friends.

But it wasn't until my long-time sound guy Pete quietly took me and Dad aside that we really understood who we were talking to. 'Guys, he's not an apple farmer,' said Pete. 'He's Steve Wozniak,

co-founder of Apple Computer. As in, the designer of the first commercially successful personal computer. The co-founder of the world's most successful computer company.'

Oh. OK.

Then Pete added, 'So I don't like your chances of getting those Granny Smiths.'

The Granny Smith apple doesn't fall far from the tree.

Not cleaning out my kid's lunchbox at the end of the term leads to a nasty surprise at the start of next term.

11.

We can embrace change and respect tradition

As a young teenager, my son Talon played in an Aussie Rules rep football team in our home area of the central coast of New South Wales. He and the other players were given the option to attend a drug-and-alcohol-awareness seminar to inform them of the negative effect substance abuse can have, particularly in association with sport. I thought this was a pretty good idea, so I volunteered to be the mum who drove the boys to the seminar.

It was held at a place called The Glen, out in Chittaway Point, a predominantly Aboriginal-based rehab centre for men over eighteen from all over Australia to recover from addiction and start building practical life skills in a culturally safe and supportive environment.

Our footy boys didn't know what to expect. They sat there in the small, simple conference room and listened intently, wide-eyed and shocked, for an hour as three tough and straight-to-the-point Aboriginal men told them all about how drugs and alcohol had fucked up their lives. These men told their stories without holding back or sugar-coating anything. They spoke of the crime they'd ended up in, the family and friends they'd lost, the opportunities gone, the violence it brought out in them and the jail time they'd endured. And it was all followed up with tea and cake.

I like this place, I thought. Real people sharing real stuff, making a real difference, and then serving tea and cake.

The whole ride home, the footy boys barely said a word, letting the reality of what they'd just heard sink in. As for me, over the next few days, I started to feel something drawing me back to that place. My inner foghorn was steering me back towards The Glen, and over the next few years I would often visit with the clients and the staff. I would bring my guitar, and we would all sit around the centre's campfire, telling stories, having singalongs, writing songs and music, sharing parts of our lives and opening up together.

I had never really experienced any substance abuse in my life. I've never been much of a drinker and neither were my parents. Drugs and alcohol have just never really been a part of my immediate world so, honestly, I had no idea what any of these men were actually going through. On one level, we were all worlds apart. But, whenever we sat around that campfire, it didn't matter where any of us were from. It didn't matter what any of us had done. It didn't matter what any of us had been through. It didn't matter how anyone had ended up there. All that mattered was that, right then, in that moment, all of our hearts were open and our judgement was left at the door.

These men were at the hardest point of their lives. Digging as deep as they ever had. From ground zero. Making an actual change in their lives. The centre drew on Aboriginal cultures in the rehab program, helping the Aboriginal men to connect back to themselves and their land, while also often opening the door and sharing the power of these traditional cultures with non-Aboriginal men with similar struggles along the way. Traditional cultures and a way of life that certainly felt much closer to my own heart and childhood than any other lifestyle or custom I had experienced as an adult.

Every gathering was genuine and authentic. All the bullshit stripped away. These men were open and real, and sometimes they didn't even need to say a word.

As I sat there around that campfire, I might have been a world apart on paper, but I felt like I had found a home of kindred spirits.

The Glen wormed its way right into my heart. On one of my first dates with my current partner (and guitar player), Brando, we chose to visit The Glen together and played songs around the campfire. Way more romantic to me than a fancy candle-lit dinner. Brando has since gone on to become a part of The Glen family as well, and works there regularly, teaching guitar and helping out.

I was also honoured to be a part of the opening of The Glen centre for women, and continue to be part of their ongoing program. My daughter and I still visit regularly and love to host big cook-ups at the centres. Brando and I spend every Christmas morning playing music for the staff and clients who don't get the chance to go home and be with their own families.

Too often, the stigma around drug and alcohol abuse overshadows the real person behind the addiction. But this place has opened my heart and my mind to connecting with people from all walks of life

and all backgrounds. It has shown me yet another powerful side of vulnerability, and how being open and real can change people's lives.

So, what started out as just a place I had to drive my son's footy team to actually became one of the most life-changing places I've ever been. And every visit to The Glen still reminds me that we don't have to be blood-related to be a family.

You never know where you'll find a family.

I was asked to sit on the panel of a 'career and songwriting' workshop along with some international songwriters and other successful artists. The host would ask questions about our careers, songwriting and music-industry experience.

On the day, the first question the host directed at me was about branding. 'Kasey, how do you approach your branding?' he said. 'How do you so successfully match your product to your brand?'

I furrowed my brow. 'What do you mean, my "brand"?' I asked naively, forgetting for a second that we were in front of an audience.

'Well, you know, your "Kasey Chambers brand"? The girl next door. The approachable, down-to-earth singer who is open and honest.'

I was still confused. 'Are you talking about my personality?' I asked.

'Well, have you chosen your brand based on your personality?' he replied.

'Mate, I don't think I've ever really thought about a brand in my whole life, let alone chosen one,' I said. 'I actually don't think I even knew I had one. Whenever I think of the term "branding", I just see businesspeople sitting around a marketing table in some corporate building, coming up with ways to sell a product. Am I a brand? Maybe I am. Geez, mate, I don't know. Sorry I'm not much help on this one.'

The audience looked as confused as I felt, and the seminar moved on. But afterwards I got thinking about it all. Maybe he was right. Maybe I was a brand? Were my songs and albums just products? It did make some sense, because I obviously market them and sell them to people …

But when I really thought about it like that, it felt so uninspiring. Breaking all of my creativity down and then labelling it as something so mass-produced just didn't sit right with me, and nor did terms like 'brand', 'product' and 'marketing'.

It kinda made me feel more like a piece of merchandise than a creative human.

• • •

All of a sudden, I started hearing this term everywhere in the music industry. Branding, branding, branding. *Does your product fit your brand? How to best market your brand! Key strategies for a successful brand.*

Had music really come to this?

Were we all just products and brands?

Now, I don't want to be someone who just fights progress and change for the sake of it, like some grumpy old man sitting on his porch with a banjo, shaking his fist at the modern world (OK, some days I kinda do wanna be him) … but I also don't want to just abandon all the things that mean something to me if they don't fit my 'brand' or sell my product. I don't want to succumb to every trend that comes along, just to keep up with what everyone else is doing.

Maybe there's a middle ground in there to find? A balance that highlights the best from both sides?

Maybe I can embrace some parts of this new world and its ideas, but still keep the traditional things that mean something to me?

And maybe I can give them all my own definition along the way? Maybe branding my creativity isn't such bad thing, if I just make sure to do it in a way that's still authentic to me?

In fact, that might just be exactly what I've been doing all along.

The brand doesn't have to come first. The creativity can determine the brand. I don't have to sit around wondering how to make my songs fit my brand. And if the songs don't fit the brand anymore, and if the brand doesn't feel like who I am anymore, then maybe it's time for a re-branding.

That's always mine to decide.

These days, I do sit on my porch a lot with my banjo, but instead of shaking my angry fist at the world I happily remind myself that:

- my inner foghorn determines my brand
- my tribe are my businesspeople
- my heart is my marketing table
- my soul is my corporate building
- my creativity is my product
- my authenticity is still always my easiest sell.

Be the black sheep when they're branding the cattle.

When I started making my next album, *Bittersweet*, Nash suggested that a guy called Nick DiDia might be a good fit for producing it. So I thought I'd do some research, look further into Nick's body of work and consider him for my next creative project ... then I saw that he'd worked with Bruce Springsteen on six records, and that was all the convincing I really needed. I'd always seen Springsteen as one of the most heartfelt and beautifully sincere songwriters in the world, so if it was good enough for Bruce it was damn sure good enough for me.

Musically, I was sold. The only other research I needed to do was to find out if he was a dickhead or not. I called up my friend Bernard Fanning. (Yep. You can call me a name dropper if you want.) We had known each other for many years, and I can't actually remember when we first met. We'd just crossed paths a lot in the music industry – at festivals, functions, awards shows and charity gigs – and had

always clicked. Our friendship quickly fell into a big brother–little sister dynamic. Eventually, we ended up singing together, recording together, writing together and becoming friends.

I knew Bernard had worked a lot with Nick on various Powderfinger albums, so I thought he could give me a good idea of what Nick would be like to work with. Well, Bernard gave him even higher praise than I could have hoped for, so the collaboration with Nick DiDia was born – and Bernard also ended up becoming a part of the *Bittersweet* album band, playing keys, guitar and harmonica, doing vocals, co-writing and helping to arrange all the songs.

The recording session for that album became one of my favourites ever. Nick was about as far away from being a dickhead as you could possibly get.

And, for fear of threatening his reputation as the hard-core frontman of one of the biggest rock bands in Australian history, I won't tell you that Bernard Fanning only drinks tea backstage. But I will say this: I've never felt anything but pure kindness and respect from this guy. He's a fucking good egg. One of the best eggs I know.

I accidentally sent a text message to his phone one day because his name and number in my phone – 'Bernie' – is right next to that of one of my best girlfriends, Bern. In the message, I shared with him all the gory details of the heavy-flow menstrual cycle I was experiencing at the time and he had the decency to never, ever speak of it again. Respect.

Real friends respect a heavy flow.

One night after a gig in Rockhampton in 2017, my roadie Worm was given a note by a sixty-seven-year-old woman from Emerald, in Queensland.

Dear Kasey, it read. *I know you must get requests like this all the time, but we run a little school in Zambia, in Africa, called Our Rainbow House and I know how special your connection with Africa is. Would you ever consider becoming an ambassador for our little school?*

I've had a lot of similar requests from different charities and fundraisers over the years, and as much as I always try to do what I can, there is no way to get to all of them. But this one stood out. And not just because of the connection my mum and I have with Africa. There was something even more. I'm not even really sure what it was, but something was drawing me in deeper. It's like my higher old mate was guiding my inner foghorn to steer me towards this place. I just had this feeling that I had to follow this path.

I had never been an official ambassador for anything before, so I didn't want to take the title and honour lightly. I did a bit of research, and learnt that the school was run by a board of a few caring people in the central highlands in Queensland. This little school was in one of the most poverty-stricken parts of Africa, the Lusaka region in Zambia, and provided education, opportunities and nutrition to fifty vulnerable children.

I decided my next step towards considering this role would be a visit to the school, to see what it was all about. Mum and I certainly didn't ever need much tempting to take another trip to Africa, so we got on a plane – three planes, actually – and flew from Sydney to Perth to Johannesburg to Lusaka, where we were met by the writer of that letter, Alison Ray.

We arrived on a Saturday, so the school wasn't open. Saturday in Lusaka was all about soccer, so we drove up to the soccer field on the edge of the compound – a big clearing of hard, hot, dusty dirt with no grass anywhere to be seen – in the beat-up old staff car. About fifteen little kids ran up to my door, cheering with excitement to see out-of-towners arrive. We certainly stood out in this community. The window on my side was broken and wouldn't wind all the way down, so the little boy closest to the car on my side – he was wearing old, ripped soccer clothes and only one dusty shoe – stood on his tippy toes to talk to me over the top of the crack in the window.

'What is your name?' he asked.

'Kasey,' I replied.

'Kasey Chambers? I am Kenny,' he said, then immediately launched into singing 'The Captain': 'You be the captain, and I'll be no one, and you can carry me away if you want to …' And as he sang, all the kids moved in closer around him, joining in, until our car was

surrounded by this incredible choir of children, singing the lyrics of my most favourite and comforting song that I have ever written.

An emotion swept over me that I cannot explain. The tears started welling up in my eyes, and my heart felt like it might burst out of my chest with love. Weeping with joy and a little confused, I wondered aloud, 'How do they even know this song? Am I famous in Zambia and I didn't even know it?'

In the driver's seat, Alison turned to me. 'Well, this was supposed to be your surprise greeting on Monday morning at the school …' She was laughing through her own tears.

She and the local teachers had taught these beautiful kids a bunch of my songs so they'd be able to sing them for me and my mum when we arrived at the morning assembly, but the kids just couldn't wait to share them.

We got out of the car, and all those children gathered around us with hugs, high-fives, songs, huge smiles, open hearts, laughter, kindness and a welcome that connected to my soul like I was being called home. I knew at that moment that this was exactly where I belonged. My heart had found another home.

• • •

I have now been the proud ambassador for Our Rainbow House for over seven years.

After that first visit, Brando and I started visiting the school regularly a few times every year to play music and write songs with the kids. Brando has taught them to play guitar, and we've served food and helped with school lessons (although I think the kids have usually taught us more than we've taught them). We've played music for the families in the nearby community.

My mum has visited again too, to give the kids craft lessons.

My eldest son, Talon, taught the whole school to play Aussie Rules football, and my second son, Arlo, taught the students to play songs on the ukulele and the guitar. Meanwhile, the little kids taught my daughter, Poet, all the local dances and braided her hair.

Brando has joined the soccer team on the weekends and been outrun by all the boys.

We've proudly cheered on the Our Rainbow House netball team in their finals.

The locals have taken us to church services, and we've heard them sing their faithful gospel songs in beautiful harmony.

One day, we even flew a makeshift studio over to the little school to record all the songs that we'd written with the students over the years. We had them all sing and play on what eventually became a fundraising CD.

The kids have taught us songs in the Nyanja language, and shared every bit of love they have in their hearts with us on every single visit.

Our Rainbow House has opened my heart in ways I've never known before.

Every time I visit, and whenever I see all those smiling little faces on our regular video calls – when we share songs and dances with each other too – I am reminded that I never need to go chasing anything at the end of any rainbow. The pot of gold is always right there in front of me.

I don't have to chase happiness.
When I listen to my inner foghorn,
she always leads me to it.

My kids and I are fans of Ed Sheeran. We've seen him live on all his Aussie tours, and being there in such a massive sea of people we've always been blown away and felt so inspired after every gig.

I remember one night when we were going to see him play, all of us were walking excitedly from the carpark to the stadium when Arlo – about nine or ten years old at the time – realised he'd left his jumper in the car. I was hurrying them along, desperate to catch the opening act, Foy Vance, also one of our favourites. Arlo started moaning that life was unfair, so Talon turned to him and said, 'Arlo! Stop your whinging. Don't you know that there are kids in Africa who don't even get to see Ed Sheeran?'

Not sure my gratitude lessons had really kicked in just yet, but I can't say he didn't at least try.

I was working on my eleventh studio album at the time. (I think it was the eleventh – I've lost count at this point.) A double record called *Dragonfly*, with one album produced by Paul Kelly and the other by my brother, Nash. I had written a lot of the songs with my beautiful friend Harry Hookey, including one called 'Satellite' that we'd both thought would sound perfect with a guest harmony by someone who sounds kinda like Ed Sheeran. So we'd started trying to think of people we knew who shared his beautiful, clean tone ... But when we failed to come up with a harmony option that felt as perfect as Ed, Harry and I started toying with the idea of actually asking him.

I'd signed back with Tony Harlow when he returned to Australia to run Warner Music – the same label Ed was signed to. Tony had been good friends with him since the early days, before Ed's major success, but I'd still never met Ed personally at this point.

Could I just ask him? What was the worst that could happen?

And my self-doubt popped up.

Self-doubt is a funny thing. It pops its head up a lot without me even noticing. It plants little seeds of insecurity in my mind and starts making me mistrust myself. It uses fear of failure and criticism to get its point across, and to stop me from putting myself out there into the unknown.

Self-doubt gave me a scenario of what would likely happen if I asked Ed Sheeran to sing with me. I would ask him the question, my self-doubt said, and Ed – in the form of the devil – would point and laugh at me condescendingly, telling me I had absolutely no right to ever ask someone of his importance and level of fame to sing with me. I was just some little country singer from outback Australia, and there was no chance of it ever happening. And, as I watched, the flames rose up and Devil Ed told me to go to hell.

OK, self-doubt, I thought. *That sounds very humiliating and embarrassing. No one wants to feel that. You're right. I shouldn't ask.*

Then my ego popped up and said, 'Kase, don't think like that ... Of course he'll wanna do it. Ed has probably been sitting at home by the phone all this time, just waiting for you to call. It's his chance to finally get you to sign his limited-edition Kasey Chambers miniature figurine!'

So, my self-doubt and ego had a back-and-forth argument for a while, each making extremely valid points, until this little thing called 'reality' (steered by my inner foghorn) jumped up and said to both of them, 'Alright, you two fuckwits. Pipe down. You are both behaving like dickheads and I've had enough. The reality of the situation is that, if you ask, there are two likely scenarios: he will say yes, or he will say no. But if you don't ever put yourself out there and just try some shit, nothing cool will ever happen. Now, get over yourselves.'

I asked.

Ed said yes.

He sounded beautiful on the song. And he is not the devil. He is human, and quite a beautiful one at that, from my brief encounter.

He did not, however, get me to sign his Kasey Chambers miniature figurine. (Too nervous to ask, probably.)

Self-doubt is a dickhead.
Ego is a dickhead.
Ed Sheeran is not.

When I ask for help, I get help. And it helps.

12.

I ain't no little girl

In 2018, I was given the honour of being the youngest female ever to be inducted into the ARIA Hall of Fame.

I was pretty shocked, to be honest. I'd been fortunate enough over the years to have been nominated for thirty-four ARIA awards and win fourteen, but the Hall of Fame was something else. I had never even thought of it as being a possibility for someone like me. I mean, how could this little country singer from the Nullarbor end up with the highest accolade in Australian music? That seemed just crazy. But, when they said they wanted to give it to me, I was damn sure gonna take it!

Years earlier, during most of my marriage, I'd thought I was doing pretty well at life and had everything sorted. At that time, I had spawned three little rugrats, was keeping a functioning house and career going (most of the time), made a few more albums, toured a fair bit in Australia and the States, and even spent a few months going to therapy and working on myself, so that should have lasted me for the remainder of my life, yeah? I figured I could rest assured that my short-lived therapy sessions had me sorted. I would forever more be totally wise and enlightened and shit.

What I didn't quite realise, of course, was that 'working on yourself' is something you need to keep doing. Something you have to practise all the time, a constant work in progress. And the effort was often the reward. But I kinda thought that I could just tick off the 'working on myself' part now and go back to 'normal' and just cruise through my life. Like a true dickhead.

And, while I wasn't paying attention, I started disconnecting from myself again. Abandoning myself to love, life, motherhood, career, perception, pressure, fatigue, expectation, blah, blah, blah … All the usual stuff most of us women regularly abandon ourselves to without even knowing it.

I was tuning out of my inner foghorn again.

I mean, I must have tuned back into her just enough to get through the divorce, but not quite enough to own my part in it, or to really behave like a mature adult very much.

Apparently, if I don't keep the conversation open with my inner foghorn, she just lets that autopilot take over. That dickhead foghorn.

• • •

Life after divorce was weird. Trying to figure out who I was now, without taking any help from my inner foghorn. Trying to get to know new parts of myself within a new family dynamic. Emotions constantly running high. Trying to protect the kids from my failure.

Pretending to myself that I was being the bigger person, while actually just being a dickhead most of the time. Playing the blame game. Trying to distract myself with shiny things and refusing to see how much I had truly lost myself again.

Blah, blah, blah.

The usual divorce stuff.

For a while, I just felt like a shell of a person. Each day just holding my head above water, trying not to drown.

The thought of being creative in any way was the last thing on my mind. I hadn't written a song, a lyric or even picked up a guitar to try to write for about eight months. And I didn't even really care.

Until one night, when I was sitting on my own on the floor beside my bed, feeling broken, exhausted and overwhelmed by the world spinning around me and a song just fell out.

I ain't no little girl. No, I ain't no little girl.
I won't cry, I won't beg, I won't plead, I won't pray,
I won't ask you to stay.
No, I ain't no little girl. No, I ain't no little girl.
I won't break, I won't bend, I won't wait,
I won't end up … with nothing to say.

I can't really remember the actual writing part of the song. I do remember sitting there in my room beforehand. I do remember picking up my guitar. I do remember how sad I felt.

And then I remember feeling like something just swept me up.

It was kinda like that feeling of weightlessness you have when you're floating in water.

It was like something took over for a little while, because it knew

I didn't have the strength to do it myself.

The song washed over me, but not like when you get dumped by a wave in the surf. It was more like the wave picked me up and carried me to where I needed to be. For just long enough to write the song. Maybe an hour.

Then it gently put me back down again, and the only difference in my life was that the song 'Ain't No Little Girl' now existed.

I still felt sad. I still felt broken, exhausted and overwhelmed.

I went back to my daily life.

And I didn't think about the song much. I didn't play it. I didn't share it. I didn't really even think it was that special.

• • •

About six months later, I started noticing that this song kept popping into my head. As I wandered around my house I would sing little parts of it to myself.

'I ain't no little girl,' as I cooked in my kitchen.

'No, I ain't no little girl,' as I drove in my car.

'I ain't no little girl,' as I cleaned my toilet.

'No, I ain't no little girl.'

This song was really not going away.

I started picking up my guitar and singing it more throughout the day. Every day. Each time I played it, I would sing with more strength and more power, and I started noticing that something was happening in my body during the song.

Connection.

Something was dropping into my body, and I was feeling connection again.

It was strange at first, but then comforting and freeing at the same time. I was connecting to myself again. I could feel my heart. I could actually feel my strength returning with every lyric that I sang. I was feeling like a woman again. But not a woman who abandons herself or blames others for who she has become. A woman who stands up for herself, owns her own shit and takes back who she truly is.

I could clearly hear my little inner foghorn again. Actually, no. I could hear my fucking loud, powerful, badass, screechy inner foghorn. She was back. It was her singing this song. To me. For me.

• • •

I started performing the song at gigs. Every time I sang it, I felt like the song was reaching deep down inside me, grabbing my strong, powerful woman and dragging her out because it knew I needed her. I wasn't being her all the time yet, but the song was helping me on my way there.

On my double album *Dragonfly*, I recorded two different versions of 'Ain't No Little Girl': one from my little inner foghorn, and one from my screechy inner foghorn. And, when the time came to choose what I would perform for my special moment being inducted into the ARIA Hall of Fame, I knew straight away what songs would be part of the performance. First 'Not Pretty Enough', and then a transition into the screechy inner-foghorn version of 'Ain't No Little Girl'. That's what would best capture the musical and personal journey of my life.

So, that's what I did, with my dad on one side of the stage playing guitar and Paul Kelly on the other playing keys. Then, Paul inducted me with a beautiful, heartfelt poem into the ARIA Hall of Fame.

I believe that the strong, powerful voice that exists inside me also exists inside all of us. She sometimes lies dormant in me when times are hard, but 'Ain't No Little Girl' brought her back to life in a way that I'd never felt before and I am grateful to the song for that.

I did not write this song. This song wrote me.

I ain't no little girl.

INTERCONTINENTAL.
SYDNEY

POEM FOR K C

When I first saw you, Kasey
You were singing in a tent
To muddy, bearded bikers
Against a pole I leant

You were singing Cripple Creek
I leant closer, getting chills
Your voice as bright as sunshine
And older than the hills

You wore a long, black dress of lace
And had those bikers cold
"Here's a great, long tale," I thought
"Already to unfold"

When we first hung out, Kasey
It was in a basement bar
A lock in after curfew
Passing 'round the guitar
Lefty, ~~[illegible]~~ Slim and Hank we sang
Gram Parsons and George Jones
The Louvin Brothers, the Stanley Brothers
Those songs were in your bones!

The first song we recorded Kasey
Was your song 'I Still Pray'
The real deal, old-time country
Has always lit your way

That real deal, old-time country
Has never been one thing
It's Blues and Holler, it's High and Lonesome
Gut bucket and an angel's wing

Those rivers all run through you, Kasey
High waters, hidden lakes
And new songs keep pouring from you
Just like a levee breaks

And all those fires burn fierce in you
Kasey, they'll never call you tame
And that is why you live right here
In my own Hall of Fame

PK

Writer's block doesn't exist. It's all just part of the process.

13.

Everything has another side

I have listened to American singer/songwriter James Taylor's music my whole life, ever since I was a kid. We even had some of his albums playing on the Nullarbor. Many years later I had the privilege of opening up a tour for him in Australia.

This was an inspiring and familiar voice to finally hear live. Sitting backstage at sound-check, I was trying to build up the courage to find an appropriate time to ask him for a photo together, when the man himself walked up to me and said, 'Would you mind if I got a selfie with you?'

'No worries, mate,' I said casually, while my heart raced to the point where I almost passed out.

Not only had James Taylor just asked *me* for a photo, but he'd even used the word selfie.

He held up his phone and took a picture of the two of us together. There is no lesson in this. I really just wanted to tell that story.

It's OK to brag sometimes.

The day I met my kids' stepmum for the first time, I was picking them up from their dad's house. It was a while after the divorce, and I knew there was another woman in my kids' lives, but I hadn't met her yet or heard too much about her.

I walked up to the door hoping the kids would just be there waiting, ready to go, so I could avoid any kind of 'pretending to be fine with this awkward situation' moment. Unfortunately, that was not the case, so I knocked on the door, now hoping that at least my ex would answer, quickly hand over the kids and off I'd go … but instead I heard a woman's voice call, 'Come in.'

I opened the door and walked inside, ready to meet an intimidating, wicked stepmother from an old fairy tale who I'd find out later in the story kept children locked up under the stairs.

This tall, beautiful woman got up from the couch. 'Hi,' she said warmly. 'I'm Emma.'

I froze for a second, and the battle within me began. My dickhead foghorn showed up first and she said, 'Put your guard up, Kase. Close up. Be wary. You don't know this person. She might be mean and nasty. Unkind and cruel. She might want to take your place as mother in your children's lives when you're not around. She might have different views from you and create her own rules for the kids here at this house that don't match up with yours. She might want to be best friends with your daughter, and they will share secrets together behind your back. She might show your kids so much attention that they start liking her more than you.'

Mmmmmmmm … These were all very likely scenarios based on standard divorces. I *should* be wary.

But then it was time for my inner foghorn to show up. She tapped me on the shoulder, cleared her throat and said, 'Take your guard down, Kase. Open up. Open your heart. You don't know this person. She might be loving and caring. Kind and nurturing. She might be *willing* to take your place as mother in your children's lives when you're not around to do it. She might have different views from you and create her own rules here at this house, and your children will get to learn so much more about life than just what you can teach them. She might be *willing* to be best friends with your daughter and they will share secrets, so Poet will always know she has someone to talk to even when she doesn't want to open up to you or her dad. She might show your kids so much attention that they feel better about themselves every day from being loved by so many beautiful people in their lives.'

My dickhead foghorn had disappeared. My heart was open. I had seen all the beautiful things that could – and would – happen in my children's lives because of this woman standing in front of me.

I leaned in towards her, she leaned in towards me – with her already open heart – and we hugged.

There's always another way to look at something.

Now, years later, Emma is also a beautiful friend of mine and one of my favourite people in the whole world. We ask each other a lot for parenting advice, and laugh a lot together when we get it wrong.

I am so grateful that our kids have this strong, kind, wise and beautiful role model in their lives. I know when they go to their dad's house they are loved, cared for and respected by their parents.

And not too long ago, Emma and Shane gave our kids a beautiful baby brother and, with their open hearts, I get to look after him every Tuesday at my house. Their baby is way cuter than any of my kids were, so that's been a little bit hard to swallow … but, aside from that, my ex-husband's partner is actually the best thing to ever happen to our divorce. And luckily Shane and I do divorce way better than marriage. We just had to go through the hard marriage to get to the good divorce.

I can't always control what choices I have, but I can control what choices I make.

'THE DIVORCE SONG'
FEAT. SHANE NICHOLSON

When my eldest son was seventeen, he called me up one morning at about ten o'clock. 'Hey, Mum,' he said. 'Guess what? I lost my virginity last night!'

We chatted away about his special night for a while, then he said, 'Actually, I'm just going to the movies with my mates right now, so

I gotta go. I'll be over later on today, and we can chat more about it then. But I really just wanted to tell you. Love you, Mum.'

I didn't realise while I was growing up how important it was to me that my parents were – and still are – so open to us talking about anything. We were always encouraged to just freely chat about everything. Even things that might have seemed a little awkward or uncomfortable to other families. We would just ask questions, bring up any topics and most of the time get fairly honest answers. I didn't always tell my parents everything, of course, but I always knew that they were there if I needed them and I didn't need to feel judged or embarrassed about bringing certain things up.

As I became older and had my own children, I started to really appreciate that my parents had given me this safe space to ask questions and learn so much about so many different things. So I tried to create that same space for my kids to be able to open up and ask about anything they needed to as well.

Of course, after incidents like when an eleven-year-old Talon came bursting into the dining room while we had people over for dinner to scream excitedly, 'MUM! I've got my first pubic hair!', I also sometimes ended up having to explain the importance of maybe finding the appropriate timing and company to bring things up in.

The more honest I am with my kids, the more honest they might be with me.

We all loved Goonga.

He got his nickname from Worm, and had joined my band for

a while and played on a few earlier records, as well as travelling on tour with us at times throughout Australia and the States. Glen was a beautiful human inside and out, and an incredible guitar player. In his later years, he also became a successful studio owner, talented photographer and graphic designer. He was husband to another one of our beautiful friends, and father of two special girls.

Everyone had always got along great with Glen on tour. In those early touring days, he and Worm would often come back from nights out with all sorts of funny stories about the random places they'd ended up and the crazy people they'd met.

But I'm sad to say that, years later, not many of us were really aware of the true extent and depth of Glen's struggles. So, when we lost him to suicide, it was extremely shocking. We were not prepared, and our hearts were ripped out of our chests.

When we first heard that Glen had gone missing, a bunch of us – his mates and his family – spent a day and a half out searching for him, hoping desperately to find him. But, finally, a police officer came out to tell us the news. Unfortunately, they had found Glen's body, not too far from the place where we were standing in that very moment.

Trying to fathom what had happened, all the friends decided to gather later on that day at Glen's house so we could be there for his wife and family. But Worm, heavy with his own pain, said to me, 'I can't go. I'll say the wrong thing. I'm no good in these situations. I'll accidentally say something stupid and make everyone feel worse.'

It took some convincing, but Worm finally agreed to come, and we all arrived together. Worm did spend that afternoon stuttering over inappropriate words, nervous beer offerings, awkward silences and uncomfortable hugs with no trace of grace or refinement – but his genuine heart spoke louder than he ever knew. The support that came from him just being there and opening his pure, rugged heart far outweighed anything that a perfectly worded, politically correct inspirational quote could have offered.

Over the next few weeks, Worm would often try to say profound and comforting things to us, only to end up with mostly swear words instead. But his true compassion and kindness shone so brightly through all those broken cracks.

Sometimes these days, I feel a bit like we spend so much of our time and energy worrying about not saying the wrong thing, about making sure we use textbook-appropriate language for difficult times. But, really, just showing up with a genuine, open heart and with a true intention will always speak the loudest, feel the most sincere and hold the most weight.

Never underestimate the essence of a Worm's heart.

In 2019, my family and I travelled through Africa with one of my best mates and lifelong family friends, Alan Pigram. Now in his late sixties, Alan is a knowledgeable and honourably discerning true bushman from the Yawuru tribe in the Kimberley region of Western Australia. He's also a well-respected musician and songwriter in the famous Aboriginal Australian band The Pigram Brothers, from the iconic town of Broome. We shared a special connection through music and living off the land.

Uncle Al has a kind, wise heart and a deep soul. He is someone who I've always looked up to. With a beautiful mixture of Filipino, Aboriginal and white Australian descent, he draws from both the bush and the sea, and embraces many different cultures throughout his free-spirited wandering lifestyle. With quiet integrity, he unassumingly shares his wisdom and advice, and never judges people for their different paths.

I've often felt guided back to my inner foghorn just by being around Uncle Al. He's one of the most peaceful and modest people I know, but he has such a strong, centred energy that has always made him an inspiring human in my life. We've known each other for a long time, and in recent years he, Brando, my dad and I made a record together, called *Campfire*. The four of us wrote a bunch of songs together inspired by sitting around the campfire, because we've always found it such a calming and grounding place to be. And, as The Fireside Disciples, we also toured together for a while throughout Australia, North America and Africa, and even visited Mexico and Jamaica.

I've always been so grateful to have Al in my inner and working tribe and to also be a part of his.

After having spent the morning dancing, singing and sharing cultures with the Maasai people of Kenya, we were now on a safari truck, experiencing the incredible sights and the wild animals of the Maasai Mara. When we came across a clan of hyenas, our Kenyan guide Sammy quietly stopped the vehicle and turned it off, so we could watch them from afar for a while. The small truck was full, with my mum, my kids, Brando, Uncle Al and I all hanging on every one of Sammy's whispered words about the hyena. We sat in silence, listening intently, but also lost in the view of these wild creatures in their natural habitat.

Then Sammy started saying something about how, if you looked

between the female hyenas' back legs (not sure why you would be doing that?), 'You'll find a thick, long, phallic-type formation with pretend testes. It's known as the pseudo penis.' And apparently, Sammy said, they use it to dominate, urinate, signal, give birth and mount the males.

Our jaws dropped and eyes widened, as we all respectfully took in the unique information being shared with us by this knowledgeable local. All of us except our always distinguished Uncle Al. He couldn't hold his giggle back. Understandable on one hand, yes. It was unusual data to get, of course.

Sammy continued, 'The hyena's clitoris is shaped and positioned just like a penis and is even capable of erection.'

The giggle got a little louder. Even my kids were managing to hold it together, but Uncle Al was struggling, despite his best efforts, to dig deep and find some kind of control within his normally calm and composed body.

Sammy glared in his direction. 'Quiet, please,' he whispered sternly. 'If you cannot control yourself, sir, I will take you back to camp and you will not return.'

Al gathered himself, while the rest of us held our respectful, serious faces and strongly avoided locking eyes with him so we'd stay that way.

Then, knowing he had our attention once more, Sammy carried on. 'The female hyena does not have an external vagina opening, because the labia are fused together to produce an artificial scrotum.'

'BAHAHAHA!' Al exploded into the loudest roaring ruckus you've ever heard, and the hyenas scurried away.

We all broke into hysterics at that moment. Except Sammy.

And I am reminded that even the most inspirational, wise and spiritual people are still just human when faced with a fake willy.

A wise man is no match for a fake willy.

In 2019, I sang a duet with Paul Kelly, called 'When We're Both Old & Mad', on his album *Songs from the South*, and we made the video together with my beautiful friend and filmmaker Siân Darling. During filming, I remember thinking ahead to the moment when the song, video and album would finally be released to the world and I would be able to share it with the public, talk about it in interviews, post about it on social media and sing the song live with Paul at his upcoming gigs. It all sounded so exciting, and it's all I could think about.

Until one moment when Siân stopped the camera rolling and said, 'Kasey, in the next take, can you pick up the piglet on the floor and gently put him back down at the door? Paul, you pat the goat on the kitchen table on your way past. Then, both of you, waltz outside together and sing, "Ooooh-lalalalalala-la," looking into each other's eyes, then come back into the kitchen and sing to the pecking chickens on the bench.'

What the fuck is my life? This is awesome!

No release date, interview or social media post could ever top the incredibly unique moment I was in right then. Why was I thinking about where it was headed? I was missing out on actually being present in one of the most unusual and wonderful experiences of my whole life.

A huge smile swept across my face. I picked up the piglet, and Paul Kelly sang into my ear while patting a goat.

Don't be a dickhead and just live in the moment.

I get to choose who I show up as every day. (Except Beyoncé. No matter how hard I try I can't seem to show up as her.)

14.

Lose yourself in unlikely places

I first heard Eminem's song 'Lose Yourself' a long time ago, when it started being played all around the world. I was instantly connected to it, and I wasn't really quite sure why. I'd grown up on pretty much just country music, although I did go through a brief heavy-metal phase as a teenager – but that was mostly just to piss my dad off. The first time I heard rap music at all I was in my early twenties.

Nash built his first makeshift home recording studio before we'd even made *The Captain*, and when a friend of my dad's was looking for somewhere for his teenage stepson and best mate to record a couple of songs that's what they used. Max and Jonathan rocked up to put down a couple of tracks, shuffling into the recording booth under our house, and I sat there in the control room with my brother while he set them up. We'd never had anyone else in our studio before, so

I was keen to listen from the other side of the double-sided glass for a change. I didn't really know what to expect.

Then they started delivering these lyrics they'd written about their young lives. Throwing narratives back and forth between them in this weird, stilted way with jolting hand movements and electric energy.

What the fuck? What the hell is this?

I had never experienced anything like it. This unusual sound filled with heart, soul, urgency and a beautiful flow, but with no melody – how were they doing this? How could they be communicating their musical story in such a different way from how I did it, but it was still connecting with me so strongly?

Their lyrics and heartfelt delivery were so real and so intense that, not only did it not need a melody in the traditional sense that I had become accustomed to, but it might have even been better without it! More immediate and powerful. So gripping and compelling.

I couldn't take my eyes or ears off them.

Fast-forward to 2021 and I had the honour of guesting as a feature on those once-teenage boys' seventh studio album, *The Sun*. As far as introductions go, mine wasn't too bad. I got my first experience of this music genre that's now dominant in Australia through rap and hip-hop OGs (my kids will kill me for using that term) Bliss n Eso.

I guess you could say that – even way back then – it was apparent that I could lose myself in unlikely musical places if it felt authentic enough. If there was connection. And it was becoming clear that this unique genre was full of connection. So, when I later heard Eminem's music for the first time, it was just the same. Every time I heard his commanding and controversial songs on the radio, I'd try so hard to not like them, to not get caught up in them. His radical and extreme lyrics were so far away from anything I would have ever put in a song of my own.

On the one hand, Eminem made me feel so uncomfortable and uneasy … but on the other, he also made me feel exhilarated and liberated. Especially when I shouted along at the top of my lungs. (Don't worry, only when I was by myself. I've never rapped in public. My kids would kill me for that too.) My reckless free spirit would get drawn in and swept up in every intense lyric and powerful performance, while my sensible and disapproving side would judge that free spirit harshly for allowing his outrageous lyrics into my heart.

It was a constant rap battle with myself.

But we can't always help who we fall in love with, right?

It was maybe a tad one-sided, but this love affair that I was developing with Eminem was real to me. No other musical artist had ever given me quite the same strong, stirring, conflicting feelings that he did.

• • •

As I broadened my musical tastes over the years – with a bit of help from my kids – I started embracing more hip-hop and rap in my playlists, and through it all 'Lose Yourself' remained a staple.

This strong, comforting song would pop up just when I needed to hear it. At times when I was subtly disconnecting from myself or my musical path, I would hear this outspoken rapper from the other side of the world telling me to dig deep and drag out my inner Rabbit. 'You've got this, Chambo.' It felt like the song was saying it directly to me.

And then one day my inner foghorn had this incredible urge to find a way to honour the song. To honour this artist and how much his approach to music meant to me. But I was never gonna rap. I had to communicate this song somehow in my own way. With my own voice. It had to be from deep within. I had to bridge my own gap between the little down-home, country sensibility that I always had deep in my musical soul and this extreme genre of music that – on paper – seemed worlds apart. In my heart, the two actually felt weirdly connected, both genres often communicating through honest, authentic life experiences.

So I picked up my banjo, strummed a minor chord (I think it was a minor chord – I don't really know how to play the banjo), and began my journey to creating my own country, folk, bluegrass version of 'Lose Yourself' by Eminem.

I had learnt and played many cover songs over the years, but this one was different. Very different. I wasn't really learning it. I was creating my own interpretation of it. And in the process, it was teaching me how to dig even deeper within myself. Every time I doubted myself and my ability to interpret this song in my own way (without sounding like a dickhead), I would just draw from the powerful lyric and the message in the song.

Something in me took over.

I'm not even really sure what it was. It's like the song had a life of its own inside me, and my job was to work as hard as I could to set it free. It was my obligation to honour it in the best way I could.

I would get up every day and play it. Practise it. Change it. Listen to it. Study it. Believe it. Rehearse it. Repeat it. For months and months, I lived in this song like my life depended on it. (My kids had to feed themselves a lot during this time.)

I don't really even know exactly *why* it was so important. My heart just needed to express gratitude for this song existing.

Now, I obviously knew that Eminem and his co-writers may have never directly intended for a banjo-playing country singer from the Nullarbor Plain to perform the song – but, to me, this was why the song was so important. This was why this song epitomised the power of music across the world. Connection – unlikely connection – between people, between artists, between places, between genres. Connection to stories, to writers, to music and mostly to ourselves.

And since then, every time that I perform this song, something unexplainable, powerful and compelling comes over me. I've never before or since been taken over so strongly by someone else's song. I even ended up including my live interpretation of 'Lose Yourself' on my latest album, *Backbone*, as the song has been such a big part of my life.

I am forever grateful for the profound advice that Slim Shady gave me (and the rest of the world, I guess) through this song, reminding us to never underestimate the power of being able to lose ourselves in the music.

Lose yourself in unlikely places.

'LOSE YOURSELF'

Brando and I ended up travelling through many different countries in Africa with our beautiful friend Matt over the years, and we racked

YOU ARE MOST
WELCOME
KASEY

up some amazing memories together before we sadly lost our friend. But the last trip we took together with him and his wife to Uganda was extra special. We got to fulfil a long-time dream to go on a trek and see incredible gorillas in the wild.

When the trip was mostly planned and only a few months away, I heard about an Australian-run organisation called School for Life that had helped to build three self-sustaining schools in Uganda. This pricked my ears up in a good way, so I dug a little deeper and my heart, my higher old mate and Google led me straight to a woman called Annabelle Chauncy. She was one of the founding members and now CEO of School for Life, and I was so moved by her story. Through building schools, Annabelle had created a way to provide education and opportunities to thousands of children and communities throughout rural Uganda. She was one of the most inspiring women I had ever heard of.

So I reached out to see if we could visit these schools to play, share and teach the kids some music on our way through to the gorilla trek. The ball started rolling, and next thing we were there in Uganda, with Annabelle in these incredible schools, sharing songs with over a thousand kids.

After our performance for the primary kids in the first school, a beautiful little girl walked up to the front of the classroom next to me and said, 'My name is Jael. When I grow up, I'm going to be a singer and travel all over the world just like you, Kasey. I've got a song to sing for you now.' And, standing there in front of me and her whole school, she sang every word of 'The Captain'.

It was one of the most beautiful sounds I had ever heard in my life.

The tears welled up in my eyes as, once again, this song connected us all, even though we came from opposite sides of the world.

For most of our time in Uganda, Brando and I ended up sharing songs and stories, and the kids would perform for us and show us every part of their beautiful schools and cultures. We taught them our songs, they taught us theirs, we danced, we laughed, we cried and we played music for all the school staff and the community.

There was so much joy. So much love.

Oh, and we did go on to do the trek too. The gorillas were amazing, but without us noticing it was the kids and their schools that became the real reason for our visit.

When I take my eyes off the prize I see so much more.

You can't save everybody but you can try.

15.

Intention needs action, and action needs intention

I never really cared too much about becoming famous. I've never really wanted to be a celebrity at all, and I haven't chosen to buy into too much of that world over the years. But I have always wanted to share my music and stories, and to connect with as many people as I can. And that is a tricky path to walk sometimes.

I guess I've had an interesting relationship with choosing a job that puts me in the public eye here in Australia to some extent. Mostly, I've just figured it out as I've gone along. Tried to not get too caught up in the bullshit, but also tried to enjoy it as much as I can. It's a fine line. One I haven't always stayed on the right side of. But it takes some pretty big ears to hear your inner foghorn *all* the time, and as I've already said I haven't always done that.

For the most part, there's not really a huge difference between who I am in my home life and who I am in my music life. If you get stuck in an elevator with me (God forbid, since I talk a lot and I'm very loud), you'll get pretty much the same person I am on stage, off stage, on TV and at home with my kids. But I am guilty of getting my head up in the clouds at times. Of thinking I'm better than I am. Of leading with my ego instead of my authentic self. And, on the other side of the scale, I've fallen apart many times because of the pressure I've felt trying to keep up with a perception of what I think the public or people around me expect from me.

At the end of the day, though, I really do fucking love my job.

I love connecting with people.

It's one of my favourite and most rewarding things to do.

I get to communicate and connect with people all the time through music, and even when it's not in a musical situation I still just love meeting people out on the road. I love chatting with people at the grocery-store checkout. I love hearing people's stories. I love getting to know people. And I love that I get to share my real self when I do it.

For a long time, this natural, organic, pure interaction with humankind was working really well for me. Then one day a friend said to me, 'Hey, have you heard of Instagram?'

Social media hadn't ever been too high on my priority list. I mean, I didn't get a smartphone until long after the rest of the world, and I only owned a laptop once for a week until I spilt a full bottle of olive oil all over it (I'd stored it in my food box on tour). I took that as a sign that technology wasn't really my thing. I'd never really done much on Facebook, I'd missed the whole short Myspace craze, and

I tried Twitter for a bit but it felt forced and annoying.

But Instagram? I kinda liked the idea of that. By this time, I had well and truly boarded the smartphone train, and I loved taking photos. Also, I was already fairly comfortable with sharing a lot of my life with strangers through music. Instagram would be just a harmless extension of that, right? An opportunity to post things about my life and music, to communicate with my fans and to see what others were up to? Free advertising and I'd get to share things I was passionate about as well?

What downside could possibly come from this?

• • •

Years went by, and I developed what I thought of as a fun, healthy, light-hearted relationship with the app.

Then, one day, another friend opened up to me about his extreme addiction to social media. Always ready to be the shoulder to lean on during hard times – especially when it's a good distraction from me having to look at my own shit – I naturally became the support he needed while he shared with me the unhealthy dependency he'd developed to trying to find validation, attention and self-worth on Facebook and Instagram.

How sad, I thought. *Imagine being so insecure that you form an attachment so extreme that you don't feel good about yourself unless a complete stranger behind a screen tells you whether you are or not? How did he get to that point? I guess someone as enlightened as me will truly never know …*

I carried on living my seemingly well-balanced life, and one day this friend innocently asked me, 'How often do you go on Instagram?'

I replied with what I thought was a fairly honest answer: 'Meh, not heaps. I post pretty regularly for work, and check a few comments every now and then, but that's about it.'

My inner foghorn made a brief, subtle appearance in the form of curiosity.

'Mmmmm … I wonder how accurate that actually is?' my inner foghorn asked. 'Are you sure you know how often you open the app, how long you stay on it, and what your true intention is behind posts and interactions?'

'Yes,' I replied. But, just to be sure, I decided to do a little experiment with myself.

First, I moved the Instagram app to a different page on my phone, just to see if I ever opened it without awareness or from habit. Then, I started checking my 'time spent' setting. I also jotted down every time I actually went in to read comments. And every time I posted something, I wrote down *honestly* what my true intention was. What was the feeling and hope I had within myself behind each post?

OK, I'm not going to reveal my exact results right now, as I'm still quite shocked, embarrassed and somewhat traumatised by how fully unaware I was about the true nature of my relationship with social media. Let's just say I opened Instagram unconsciously waaaaaay more than I ever imagined, stayed on it for much longer than I ever thought, had so much more of my validation and self-worth attached to it than I would have ever cared to admit – to myself or anyone else – and my intentions for posting were often not quite as honourable, innocent or even honest as I had convinced myself they were.

This was fucking hard to un-know.

Here's what I learnt: every moment of every day, I am faced with the option to give my time, energy and self-worth away to social media, the people behind it, their opinions, their beliefs, their thoughts, their points of view, their perceptions, their theories and their judgements – but, no matter how much they wanna take it all from me, it's still always my choice whether I give any of it away.

Break your own habit of being a dickhead.

I celebrated the twenty-year anniversary of *The Captain* in 2019 with a three-month tour around Australia, and as part of it I performed at Bluesfest, the Byron Bay blues and roots festival.

I'd been attending that festival every single year – both on and off stage – since 1998, when I first went as a back-up singer for Buddy Miller. The year after that first gig, Bluesfest promoter Peter Noble had given me my own gig. (He and his family also went on to become my good friends, and I sang at Peter's wedding when he married his beautiful wife, Dyah – my partner and I wrote the song 'For Better or Worse' for their special day.)

It was at Bluesfest in 1999 that I'd made my first appearance at any music festival under my own name, Kasey Chambers. That same year, I also played a set with The Dead Ringer Band. So this festival symbolised my transition from the family band to my solo career. It took a little piece of my heart every year, and Easter time in my mind had quickly become much more about music, love and Hungarian snap-fried bread than any kind of resurrection of Christ. And I went on to play that festival more times than any other female artist in the world.

Back when I was only a couple of months off releasing *The Captain* album, I recorded a cover of the 1995 Ben Harper song 'Another Lonely Day' for one of the B sides. Ben Harper was headlining the festival that year, and was my main priority to see perform.

Worm, Nash and I stood in that audience swept up in every moment. Ben's unassuming but commanding performance on that stage took me to a place of pure inspiration, and filled me with the encouraging certainty that I had definitely chosen the right path. The path of music. A path so powerful in connection that everyone in that sea of thousands had been lifted by Ben's beautiful, open heart and music.

And, twenty years after that life-changing gig, as I was preparing to celebrate the anniversary of my first and most poignant record, Ben Harper was once again headlining the festival. So, with an open heart (and a little help from my friend Peter), I asked Ben if he would do me the honour of helping me to celebrate by singing 'Another Lonely Day' with me.

He said yes.

He said he'd be honoured.

And he also asked if I would sing with him at his gig.

As I walked out onto that stage, I remembered that incredible moment twenty years earlier when I'd stood in that audience looking up at one of my biggest musical inspirations. And now, there I was, singing my little heart out right there next to the same beautiful man.

Dreams absolutely fucking do come true.

'FOR BETTER OR WORSE'

When I think back to making all my favourite albums – the ones that I really feel connected to – and why it is always such a special moment to finally hear the fully mixed and mastered end product, I can see that it isn't so much about how the album turns out or what it sounds like in that final listen. What matters is that it is a *record* of the beautiful experience I had while I was making it.

Writing the songs. Working with incredible musicians who I connect with personally as well as musically. Hearing my songs come to life in a new way for the first time in the studio. The new and unexpected ideas that a producer opens up in my heart. The cook-ups we have after the session has finished each day. Hearing the different interpretations of my songs when the musicians connect to them for the first time. Experimenting with different instruments and sounds with people I trust and respect. Listening to the stories that are sparked from the lyrics. The takes we have to re-do because the studio dog farts and it smells so bad we can't keep playing.

The laughter, the tears, the magic. Even the stupid, petty arguments that my brother and I have followed by the heartfelt hugs we inevitably still always share to make up.

If the recording experience is beautiful, then of course I want to capture it. Of course I want to have a record of it to share.

These days, when I think about making my records, I don't spend much time or energy thinking about what end product I want to come up with. I just create a recording experience that interests and excites me. I think about working with musicians who inspire me, and about places and environments that make me feel alive. I choose producers who I feel I will connect with, and then I love letting my songs just take on a life of their own.

The purpose of making albums, for me, really lies in the experience we have along the way. All I really need is for the finished product to be a record of that.

Making a record is really just about making a *record.*

One day my daughter, Poet, and I were getting ready to head out to the shops to get the groceries. She came downstairs from the bedroom dressed in the same dirty clothes she'd been wearing all morning and all the day before. And I mean dirty. The afternoon before, she had been outside playing in the dirt and mud, and there was also an added bolognaise stain from dinner that night.

I said, 'You can't wear that, Poet. You'll have to go put some clean clothes on.'

'But this is my favourite T-shirt,' she begged, 'and I'm going back outside to play when we get home from the shop!'

'Well, you still have to go get changed,' I said. 'You have to wear clean clothes to the shop.'

'But why, Mum?' she said. Not in a disrespectful way, more inquisitive, wanting to know my reasoning.

So I decided I would gather up that reasoning and share it with my daughter, as the wise parent who obviously knows better than her. Then I'd hurry her up to get changed into more appropriate clothing, and off we'd go to get the groceries.

First, I asked myself the question she had so innocently posed: 'Why don't I want her to wear dirty clothes to the shop?' And my initial answer was going to be …

'Because it's one of the general rules of life. We dress nice and look clean and appropriate when we go out in public.'

That seemed fair.

Not really an answer, though ... I was just stating that we do it. And that really wasn't a reason why. So I decided to look a little deeper. Actually why? Why would it really and truly bother me if we went to the shops and Poet had dirty clothes on?

Honestly, as much as I didn't want to see it – and certainly didn't want to admit it to myself – the truth was, I would feel like other people (particularly other mums) in the grocery store might look at us, see Poet, judge her for being so dirty, then look at me and judge me. *What kind of mum is she?* they'd think. *Letting her kid go out in public looking like that. Doesn't she do her laundry?*

This hit me like a tonne of bricks.

Not only because I liked to think of myself as someone who didn't care too much about what other people thought (which I was obviously in denial about), but even more importantly because I realised that I was basically telling my nine-year-old daughter that *she* should feel as though her appearance was getting judged before she even left the house. She should change her appearance to prevent that judgement, and conform to what everyone else thinks that she should look like.

And, even worse, I was telling my daughter that she was not good enough just the way she was to go out in public with her mum.

Fuck. My heart sank.

Now, this might all sound a little dramatic and overthought, based on the fact that it was just one little chat about a dirty old T-shirt, but it got me thinking. I started to imagine the amount of times in my life as a mother that I'd had similar conversations with her. And with my other kids.

I had always believed and even said out loud to my kids, 'Don't take on judgement from others. Choose your own definition of beauty. Don't worry about what people think of you. Be yourself. Don't let fear stop you from being you.'

But were my actions always matching up with my intentions?

Maybe it was time to check in with myself and see how much I was unconsciously conditioning my kids through the little things I did and passed off as 'good parenting'.

Truth: My kids are dirty sometimes. A lot of the time.

Truth: I don't always get around to doing the laundry. Sometimes because I'm busy, and sometimes because I just can't be fucked.

Truth: My kids are loved.

Truth: My kids are nurtured.

Truth: My kids never have to try to look or be perfect in any

way, and they never need to change who they are in order to please another person.

So why the fuck did I care if some stranger at the grocery store thought I wasn't a good mother?

In the deepest part of my heart, I know I am a good mother. I fuck up a lot, make mistakes, of course, but I know where my intentions are.

The thing is, though, intentions won't do all the work for me. My actions have to actually match up with them, before I get on my high horse and tell my daughter the rules of life and why we must abide by them.

So I sat Poet down, apologised for my misguided request, walked her through the steps of my life-changing epiphany in detail, and gave her credit for the inspiring question that she had asked.

She rolled her eyes at me and said, 'So, can I wear the T-shirt?'

'Yes, chicken. You can wear whatever you want.'

It's not enough to just think it and say it. My actions have to match up with it too.

I can learn something from everyone.

16.

Let your true character shine brightest in shit times

Just before the pandemic hit, I had already gone into some kind of lockdown.

In the year prior, as well as an amazing anniversary tour for *The Captain*, I had done a promotional tour, three working trips to Africa and squeezed in a full American tour with my whole extended family. I had burnt myself out, and I was really ready for a rest. I was going through some personal struggles, and Brando and I were having some relationship problems – we'd ended up in couples' therapy, which then turned into singles' therapy for a while so we could figure out who we were separately before we chose who we wanted to be together.

Then the pandemic took over, and suddenly everyone's life looked very different. The jobs considered a luxury were understandably the first to go and the last to return, and, even though I didn't have too many gigs booked in or the financial struggles that others had at the time, it was still very strange to all of a sudden be out of work.

Earlier on in my life, I'd had a lot of different jobs. Cleaning houses, motel rooms ... Actually, that's pretty much it. For most of my adult life, being a singer and a performer was all I'd ever done. It's all I'd ever really wanted to do. I think I was just born to be a performer. I mean, I smile when I open the fridge because the light comes on. Being a performer was all I'd ever really known. But suddenly that was all gone.

Even without knowing how long the lockdowns would last, realistically I knew that playing music to people at gigs in the way that I had done my whole life was not coming back in a hurry.

I had to start asking myself, 'Who am I?'

Who am I without being a singer? Without being a performer? Without gigs? Without playing to an audience? Without my job?

Could I answer these questions?

I guess I had to.

I had to start reminding myself that being a singer is not who I am. It's something that I do. Something that I choose to do.

Yes, it's something that I love to do, and it fills my heart and soul in every breath, but it's not all I have. It's not all I am.

I am grateful for the gift of singing and performing, but I also know that gift can be taken away as quickly and easily as it was given to me in the first place. And I guess I'd like to think that, if I lost my voice tomorrow, I wouldn't lose my whole identity. I need to remember that there is more to me.

I get to define myself as a lot of different things – and the more that I get those things from within, the less I give my identity away to anything or anyone else.

I am not a singer. I sing.

I am a creative. A creative who shares that creativity by singing and performing. Creativity is within me, beyond my voice, my gigs, my audience, my job. My creativity is endless and untouchable. Nothing can take it away.

But when my job was actually taken away for a while, I really had to remind myself of that. I had to remember I still had so much more creativity to draw on. Songwriting, cooking, clothing design, home decor, recording, playing guitar, singing without an audience, writing, coming up with ways to entertain the kids during lockdown. Now all that takes creativity indeed.

I am not a singer. I sing.

Like a lot of us mums do, I have also had to remind myself to apply this same approach over the years to being a mother.

After I had children, I would sometimes fall into the trap of defining myself as only being a mother. Often feeling guilty when I did things for myself, or feeling like a complete failure as a person when I made parenting mistakes. Which was a lot!

I love being a mother with all my heart and soul, and I'm so grateful to have the chance to be one, but I want to make sure it's not my whole identity. One day, my kids won't even need me anymore. (I'm sure they'll still pop in for food and money sometimes.)

When my eldest son turned twenty, he moved to Perth, on the other side of the country, to follow his dreams. (Maybe to have a break from his family too.) Who was I without him? Who was I without him needing me every day?

And who am I going to be when *all* my kids move out and don't need me anymore?

Can I actually answer those questions?

I guess I absolutely have to, because it's inevitable.

I want to show my kids – in actions, not just in words – that we can all define ourselves with so many different things. And the more that those things come from true, soul-filling places within you – instead of from outer expectations and things controlled by other people and circumstances – the more you can truly feel like a whole person. But the best way to teach my kids this is to live it myself.

I believe my job as a parent is not to do everything for my kids. Not to protect them from everything. Not to make all their decisions for them. Not to shelter them from hard times. Not to sugar-coat everything and give them the impression that life is always fair and they will always get what they want.

I'm trying to nurture them, to teach them to be able to do things for themselves, to protect themselves, to think for themselves, to be ready for hard times. And I'm trying to show them how to handle those hard times as best they can, how to learn from their mistakes when they sometimes fuck it all up.

For me, my main job as a parent is to show my kids how to tune in to their own inner foghorns and let that lead the way to their true selves. They might not choose to do exactly what I want them to do but that's not mine to decide. I want them to define their own identities. Like I am defining mine. Still, every day.

I know the day will come when they all walk out the door and don't need me to mother them anymore. But I don't want to watch my whole identity walk out that door with them.

I will always be their mother, and they know I will always be there for them, no matter what. (Unless I'm on the toilet. Then leave me alone.)

I won't let one thing become my whole identity.

For a little while during the start of the pandemic, I felt like I was able to understand enough of what was going on out in the world to compassionately accept the rules put into place. I could embrace the lockdowns enough to rest, and use the time to get to know myself again and I actually thought I was mostly doing OK. Until home-schooling hit. Then, I pretty much lost my shit every day for a bit.

I certainly developed a newfound respect for teachers, but decided I was definitely not ever cut out to be one in the sense of providing a conventional education. Especially given my own level of schooling had reached its height when I turned fifteen halfway through Year 10, my complete incompetence when it comes to technology, and my lack of patience. So my partner and I, still holding things together so far, ended up making an executive household decision: home-schooling would now mostly consist of cooking classes, music workshops, surf lessons and more family time.

This suited us much better. And soon we started seeing that there were much bigger things going on out in the world, anyway. We eventually realised that everyone on the planet was going through something extremely significant and unlike anything we'd ever experienced before. Something that was beautifully linking us together in one way, and callously dividing us all in another.

Meanwhile, each and every one of us was left to also deal with our own personal struggles at home, battles with health and finances for some people, and a shitload of amplified inner fear. All around the world, every day, the only familiar feeling was guaranteed uncertainty.

Sometimes, getting through hard shit with dignity is just making your bottom line to never steal one single roll of toilet paper from an old lady.

I guess living through that first year of lockdowns, home-schooling, intense remote therapy, re-evaluating life, no work, no travel, the threat of the end of the world and sharing a bathroom was either going to make or break a relationship between two people.

Brando and I were making it so far, slowly getting through some relationship stuff that took time, work and energy, which actually seemed somewhat easier in lockdown. Both of us knowing how healing nature can be, we decided to move to a bushland property out of town. A fresh start, a natural environment, country life and some space.

We also wanted to eventually build a recording studio and music retreat on a bit of land. (The Rabbit Hole Recording Studio became a reality a year later and brings us so much joy. Brando handles most of the music and the technical side of things, and I get to put my other favourite hobby to good use: cooking. All catering done by me.)

Despite our age gap leaning the other way, Brando was generally way more mature than me most of the time. Much more traditional than me. He had even decided not to own a smartphone anymore, and went back to an old flip-top phone so he wasn't living his life through a screen. I admired this. For him. If I'm honest, the thought of no smartphone was, for me at this point, a tad confronting and caused a little light hyperventilating. (Note to self: something I should probably bring up in therapy some time.)

Anyway, we sold our house and bought another one and we all moved out of town to some acreage. Given my extreme passion for (bordering on obsession with) wabi-sabi style home decor, I took over most of the interior-design decisions. I pretended to let Brando be involved every now and then, and he pretended to not be aware that I was only pretending to let him be involved. A match made in heaven.

We had just moved in and for the fifteenth day in a row I was doing my usual 'change all the decorative ceramic pots around to different spots in the house' routine as Ondara sang 'Torch Song' to me in his mixed Kenyan/British/American accent from my iPhone when Brando came into the room and said, 'Hey, I've got a "new house" request that would really mean a lot to me. I would love for all of us to start eating dinner together as a family every night. Around the dining table. No phones. No TV. No screens. No technology. Just us as a family. Connecting. In person. Real conversation. As people.'

Now, I'll be honest. I said, 'That's a great idea, honey. Let's do it. I love it.' And I did love it … in theory. But I kinda thought we'd just do it for a few weeks, then fade back into our old routine of eating at different times, teenagers staying in their rooms, phones popping up, kids whinging that it was boring to eat together, TV shows becoming more important, the convenience of the family doing their own things separately taking priority, and the sincere request becoming nothing more than a distant memory.

I couldn't have been more wrong.

From the first night we started our new dinner ritual, our family came together and happily created some of the best times we have ever had. Times filled with beautiful food, loving energy, roaring laughter, streaming tears, heartfelt conversations, pointless conversations, inspiring disagreements, heated arguments, loud farting, inappropriate swearing, family meetings, shared stories and thought-provoking discussions about which superhero is the greatest (Spider-Man, by the way). A real connection filled up all of our hearts every night. Every time we sat around that table, we were together. We were all just together. Nothing else mattered. Even the kids loved it!

We were connecting as humans, in person.

Even now, years later, we still all eat dinner around that table almost every night when we are home. There's been a few things to work around – since Talon has moved to Perth now, he misses out a bit, Arlo works some nights, and Poet had dance classes for a while (we ended up having to cancel them because of the return of those damn radioactive spiders, of course) – but we make the effort whenever we can. We still talk, laugh, cry, argue and connect around that table.

We also open up our dinner-time gatherings to extended family, the kids' friends, fellow musicians and neighbours. We still have the no-phone, no-screen rule no matter who is joining us, but sometimes a board game or card game evolves. One night when my mum was with us, Arlo chose family dinner as the time to introduce us all to this new card game we hadn't yet heard of. It was called Cards Against Humanity. A party game in which players complete fill-the-blank statements, using words or phrases printed on playing cards that might typically be described as offensive, risqué or politically incorrect.

I don't think Brando ever knew how many beautiful memories his well-intended, traditional house request would create. And he probably never expected to one day sit at that table and listen to his seventy-year-old mother-in-law say, card in her hand, 'My superpower is … queefing.'

• ••

Because of the lockdowns, I obviously ended up not being able to play many gigs for a couple of years. And yeah, yeah, yeah, 'my job doesn't define me', 'music is not my identity', 'my self-worth is not all about being a singer', blah, blah, blah, but the truth is, I just really missed singing and playing to people.

I knew it was likely to still be a long way off before we would play the sorts of big festival gigs or national tours that we'd so fortunately become accustomed to before Covid, but I still just longed for a little bit of connection again with people through music.

We had reached the point in New South Wales where restaurants were allowed to open again, but only half full, so that no one was seated too close to anyone else. Brando, my dad and I decided we would safely start up a small regular gig at a friend's local restaurant called The Dart n Feather. Legally, we could fit about sixty people inside, so we booked it in every week for a month. And, a bit like Dad and I had done all those years earlier, we had a low-key Thursday-night jam for the next few weeks. The three of us would turn up each week with an acoustic instrument, one condenser microphone for us all to sing and play around together, and with our hearts ready to connect again we began The Dart n Feather fireside sessions.

We didn't plan a set list. We just played whatever popped into our heads. Whatever direction our musical wind blew us in, that is where we went. We would play old country songs, and often sing the wrong lyrics and mess up the chords. We would play heartfelt, romantic Springsteen covers, and the whole room would fall in love. We would play the first half of many Dylan songs, because there were too many verses to learn the whole lot. We would share stories from our childhoods and our musical history, and try out new original songs we'd written just days prior. We would attempt obscure requests from the small but regular crowd even if we didn't know the song, and we would sometimes laugh all the way through. Sometimes we would cry all the way through.

Sometimes we sounded beautiful, and sometimes we sounded fucking horrible. We would get so lost in the moment that some songs would go on and on for far too long, and sometimes we couldn't even make it to the end because we were laughing so hard.

But none of it mattered. Because *all* of it mattered.

For those few hours every week, all that existed for us was what was going on in that room. We were all connecting again. We were all realising how important music had been in our lives, and how much we had all missed it.

So, what started out as just a few weeks turned into an entire year of Thursday nights when every one of us in that room, for a few hours, got to take a break from the craziness going on out in the world, just unite again and feel like everything's gonna be alright.

Music was bringing us back together.

Every time we tried out a newly written song, it was like we were sharing it with our closest friends. The crowd would join in like a choir on songs they'd never even heard before.

My kids and other musician friends would come along and jam with us. We got to know the audience members by name, and they shared stories of their lives with us. We started feeling like everyone in that room was family.

Every week, we all came in from different places, different backgrounds, different experiences. We all had different beliefs and opinions about all the complicated and conflicting things going on out there in the world. Some of us believed one thing, some of us believed another. But every Thursday night, every one of us put all of that aside and just came together with an unspoken love for music and bonding with people again. It didn't matter what 'side' you were on. Thursday night at The Dart n Feather reminded us all that, deep down, we were always on the same side.

The side of connection.

Those fireside sessions reminded me, more than ever, that unity is not about everyone having the same beliefs and opinions. For me, true unity is about everyone coming together with love and respect in spite of their different beliefs and opinions.

Just because I have a strong opinion doesn't mean everyone has to hear it.

'DART N FEATHER'

Doing soul-filling things fills up my soul.

17.

Live your own dream life, not someone else's

When we finally got back to actually touring again in 2022, I was sitting in a Sydney airport lounge waiting for a flight when a feeling of emptiness crept up inside me. I looked around and I just felt a bit lost.

I immediately tried to cover up the feeling, quickly reminding myself of the privileged situation I was in. How could I possibly feel empty and lost with all this around me? I was finally back playing gigs all around Australia, just like I had been lucky enough to do for so many years of my life. Fortunate enough to be travelling to gig destinations all over the country, waiting in airport lounges, conveniently flying into cities and towns, picking up hire cars, checking in to nice hotels, getting to sound-check, heading back to the hotel for room-service dinner, back to the venue for the gig, back to the hotel to sleep, and then up early and straight back to the airport for another flight home or on to the next town for the next gig. What an incredibly convenient and comfortable life I had earnt for myself. And my kids, who were still travelling with me on some of the trips, got to hang out in airport lounges too, zoning out on their iPads during flights and seeing the inside of some very fancy hotel rooms all over the country.

I sat there reminding myself of how lucky I was to have created all this through music. It was the exact lifestyle that I had worked so hard to acquire. And, more importantly, I had to remind myself that this was the absolute dream life for most musicians all over the world. But ... was it mine? Was this *actually* my dream life?

I felt a bit out of place. Grateful, but out of place.

Along with my empty feeling, some underlying anxiety popped up. *Something's not right.*

I started thinking back to my childhood. Often, when Nash and I were kids, our parents would use the money they'd made after the hunting season was finished each year to take our family in an old caravan and four-wheel drive throughout different parts of Australia. We would stay in cheap bush camps, parking bays on the side of highways or down random dirt tracks. We'd park up at relatives' properties, swim in natural swimming holes along the way, stumble across spectacular waterfalls in secluded areas, visit Aboriginal communities and make friends with the kids, fish for dinner in winding rivers and on ocean shores, and get to know locals in outback towns and remote roadhouses. I would meet kids my age in caravan parks, then meet up with them again in other towns.

What memories am I making for my kids these days? I found myself

wondering. *Am I shaping them through airport lounges and an iPad?*

Was this helping to shape who they would become? Was I really showing them how to let their free spirits fly?

When my kids were younger, we all travelled together on tour and had so much fun. A few planes but lots of road-tripping too – tour buses, days off doing fun things in random towns. Now, things were different. They were easy. They were comfortable. They were very convenient.

But are beautiful memories ever made from convenience?

I looked around the lounge, my little inner foghorn begging to be heard, and I realised at that moment that I was not living my authentic life anymore. I had taken on someone else's idea of a dream life, but it wasn't mine.

Beautiful memories are not made from convenience.

Throughout my life, I've had many times when I have suffered from anxiety. That thing in my body that makes it feel like two giant hands are twisting my chest and trying to wring me out like a wet towel. Sometimes, anxiety sits in the background of my day like a storm quietly brewing beneath my skin, just waiting for a legitimate but unrelated reason to surface and take over. And sometimes it erupts as a full-blown panic attack that takes over my whole body, to the point where I think I'm having a medical emergency and I call an ambulance. (Yep. Pretty embarrassing diagnosis to get from a paramedic when you're under the impression you really know yourself and have your shit together.)

As I look back over these anxious times in my life, I realise that pretty much every time I've ever felt like this, it was when I was not living as my true self. It was when I was trying to be something I am not. Always at times when I was hiding parts of my true self out of fear of judgement, or when I was in a bad habit of talking down to myself and letting the noise and doubt from the outside world get inside my head. Basically, it was when I was not tuning in to my inner foghorn.

It was when I realised this that I started to wonder whether, maybe, my anxiety *was* my inner foghorn. Maybe it was her way of trying to tell me that something wasn't right. Maybe I didn't have to fear the anxiety, but should instead listen to what it was telling me – to make some changes, to redirect myself towards my authenticity.

But how, I wanted to know, was I possibly going to calm this overactive, frantically busy, anxious mind of mine for long enough to be able to hear what my inner foghorn was trying to tell me? And, honestly, did I even want to hear what she might have to say?

'Meditation,' she said. 'Try it.'

'Meh, I really don't do that,' I replied. 'It's not really for me. Not my thang. I've tried it before. Certainly tried it enough to be able to say I can't do it, it didn't work for me.'

Becoming a perfect, enlightened, calm meditator just seemed so far out of my realm. The thought of sitting still, clearing my mind, letting go of my thoughts, turning off from distractions, calming my body, targeting my attention, embracing the quiet, and turning my mind off … or was it turning my mind *on*? Focusing, or was it *not* focusing? Concentrating, or was it *not* concentrating?

Fuck. OK, I wasn't even sure what meditation was. No wonder I couldn't fucking do it.

But – and this was maybe the hardest part (and most convenient excuse) of all – where the fuck would I find the time? I was certainly not going to cut into my important downtime watching gruesome true-crime documentaries on Netflix at the end of a long day. Who would solve all those murder mysteries if I wasn't helping from the other side of the screen?

It all just sounded a bit too hard.

But my inner foghorn kept tapping away at me. Kept popping up with anxiety and unease to tell me something still wasn't sitting right within me. (The negative murder-mystery energy I was filling my head with *might* have been directly related, but one step at a time.)

I've never been one to jump to medication unless absolutely necessary, so I really wanted to at least explore the avenue of trying to fix this anxiety from the inside out first, before putting something from the outside in. I started thinking it might be time to give meditation one more try – but maybe I needed a new approach. *What would my little inner foghorn say about my failing attempts at meditation? Mmmmm?*

She would probably say, 'Why are you trying to be the perfect, enlightened meditator anyway? Why are you putting so much pressure on yourself? Who told you what meditation has to be like for you? And why are you letting someone else tell you how you're supposed to feel?'

And, if the relationship I had with meditation was like my relationship with music and creativity, what would I tell myself? Firstly, I wouldn't be so hard on myself. I would speak to myself with more compassion and understanding. And I wouldn't really worry too much about what other people expected from me. I'd say, 'Here is my version. You don't have to like it or agree with it.'

So maybe I could come up with my own definition of meditation?

No one was going to score me at the end on how well I did. No one was going to hand me a trophy if I did it right, or take away my meditation licence if I did it wrong. Maybe I just needed to stop overthinking it so much and practise it a bit more, instead of just giving up. Maybe I needed to let it naturally just become what it was meant to be, for me?

Now, that sounded a little easier.

I guess I also had to ask myself, realistically, *why* I was talking myself out of meditation anyway? Why was I really fighting against it?

Was it because being able to say 'I am not a good meditator' or 'I've tried but I can't do it properly' was actually a pretty good, easy excuse to not have to make time in my day to do it?

Was it because truly spending some real time with myself was a bit confronting?

Was it because trying it, and being guided by all these superior spiritual guides who seemed to always have everything sorted, sometimes just made me feel small and stupid?

Was it because, if I did sit still for too long, all this hard shit might come up that I didn't really want to see or face? Stuff that might make me realise how much I was *not* connected to myself and *not* living as my true self, and then I wouldn't be able to ignore it anymore?

Was it because it might feel uncomfortable?

'OK, Chambo,' I said to myself. 'Time to get real. Life isn't always about being comfortable. Maybe it's time to throw out all the rules you've heard and attached to meditation. Throw out all the things you think you're "supposed" to feel or get out of it, and just be. Sit quietly with yourself and just be. Do this for yourself. Not for anyone else. Just do it for you. For your inner foghorn. She is there waiting.'

So every day, over and over, I would put my headphones on and listen to a guided meditation (total silence was a bit too confronting to start with) and I would just sit there. And sit there. And sit there.

If my mind went crazy, then that was OK. If I couldn't concentrate, then that was OK. If I ended up laughing, then that was OK. If I ended up crying, then that was OK. If shit came up that made me feel uncomfortable, then that was OK.

I didn't have to fix any of it. (I could work on that later, usually with my always patient and brutally honest but brilliant therapist, Lisa.) I didn't have to analyse it.

I could just be.

If I couldn't focus properly, then that was OK. If I ended up just writing my shopping list in my head, then that was OK. All I really had to do was show up for myself and give myself time to just be. Sometimes five minutes, sometimes thirty. Whatever. Just time. That's all. Every day.

I started getting up half an hour earlier in the morning so that I could start my day with meditation. I started replacing my true-crime documentaries with meditation and podcasts about uplifting and self-empowering things. I started listening to positive affirmations while I cooked, cleaned, drove and did my grocery shopping. I started filling some of the gaps in my day with meditation instead of scrolling on Instagram.

And after a while – quite a long while of practice, discipline and constant self-reminders to just keep trying – everything started to feel different. Meditation started flowing with ease. I started feeling lost in it. Hell, I was even starting to look forward to it! What the fuck? Meditation? And me? Were we becoming … friends?

It felt like I had developed special superpowers and I could transport myself to this magical little enchanted place inside myself at any time that I wanted to during the day. Kinda like the adult version of using your imaginary superpowers when you're a kid. A place where there was no judgement, no pressure, no time, no expectation, no rules, no conditioning, no stress and, eventually, no anxiety. The perfect home for a free little spirit like mine to visit every day. And she needed it – I had neglected her a lot.

I was getting swept up in it, I was actually sometimes even enjoying it, feeling calm and grounded in it. I even started discovering that, after most meditations, I was actually bringing some of that grounded feeling back with me into the 'real world' – and sometimes even carrying it with me through the whole rest of my day!

It took a little while and a bit of searching to find the meditation guides I really connected with, but I was getting there (with the help of the calming sincerity of Mooji, the grounding humour of David Gandelman and later finding the peaceful magic in John Butler's meditation album, *Running River*). My stress and anxiety were fading, slowly being replaced by a peaceful certainty that reminded me that, most of the time in the moment, everything actually is alright.

Any time stress and anxiety would pop up again, it was like I had these magical tools within me for dealing with them in a more reasonable and healthy way than just letting them and my thoughts drag me around for the rest of my day.

Everything felt lighter and more beautiful. Hard things seemed easier to handle and took less of my energy and time. Everything flowed more, and my free little spirit no longer felt as trapped and silenced. She even started being creative again.

I now start every day with meditation, do a couple more throughout the day, sometimes some breath work, and I listen to positive affirmations and mindful, purposeful podcasts on long drives. I do this instead of filling my head with every fact there is to know about what makes a serial killer's mind work – even though I'm sure that *would* be handy information to have for easily spotting a serial killer on the street. I think, at this stage in my life, it's working a little better for my mental health to make a bit more time and space for positive thoughts and energy. And maybe not only for my mental health but also my physical health. I mean, realistically, if negative vibes cause stress, and stress causes physical strain, then positive vibes would have to have a positive effect on my body, right? My own little healing plan. Inside and out.

So, for now, I have chosen to make meditation a part of my daily life. Sometimes I get totally lost in it, sometimes it stills my scattered mind, sometimes I feel peace and calm, sometimes I remember an email I forgot to send from seven years ago, sometimes I feel my life change dramatically, sometimes I rewrite my shopping list in my head, sometimes hard shit comes up and I feel uncomfortable, sometimes I feel enlightened and sometimes my daughter lifts up one of my eyelids and whispers, 'Do we have any waffles left?' But, no matter what, after meditation I *always* feel better.

Meditation might actually be better for my mental health than watching gruesome true-crime documentaries on Netflix.

I decided to trade in the frequent-flyer lifestyle for a caravan and a four-wheel drive and start road-tripping again. It wasn't hard to get Brando, who also played guitar in my touring band, on board – he always loved a big drive over a flight anyway. And, even though my kids had never travelled in a caravan before, they loved an adventure and thought they might get out of a bit of school, so they were also easily convinced. My heart was singing with the thought of getting back to a more organic, simpler way of life. One that matched up more with my childhood.

OK, we weren't exactly going to be roughing it – no old homemade van or swags like my childhood – but by the end of the year we had cancelled all our flights and ordered a 22-foot off-grid Kokoda caravan. I hadn't towed much in my life, so the size of the caravan could have seemed a little daunting for me if I'd let myself think about it. But I was so distracted by the excitement of being able to decorate the inside when it arrived that I wasn't really worried about that. Yet.

First and foremost, though, I had to at least think about getting a vehicle big enough to tow the van. Yeah, most people probably would have wisely sorted the vehicle before ordering the van, but I got a bit ahead of myself. And I soon discovered I was going to need something fairly heavy duty, as it was a 4.5-tonne van.

I've never been into cars much, so I figured just talking to a few people who had done some towing themselves might be a good place to start. My dad mentioned Chevy might be worth looking in to, but honestly I wasn't even sure what a Chevy looked like. Next, I called my mate Trevor from Kokoda – I had made a bit of a habit of bugging him with caravan questions, but he hadn't blocked my number yet. A quick two-and-a-half-hour phone call (one of our standard chats) later, I left with his high recommendation: a Chevy Silverado sounded pretty good to me. I sat down at my kitchen table and started googling images to see what these vehicles looked like.

Fuck. They are big!

I am a fairly small human. Only 159 centimetres tall (or short), and a relatively small build. I also didn't even learn to drive a normal car until I was thirty years old.

This truck might be a bit beyond what I can handle, I thought. *Will my feet even reach the pedals? And will I be able to see over the dashboard?*

Fear crept up. Self-doubt crept up. A little vomit crept up.

I looked at more and more pictures of these big trucks, and found some comparing them to normal-sized cars. *Holy moly!* It was starting to feel very fucking overwhelming. Fear and self-doubt had officially moved back in, and they were actually making a lot of sense. My inner foghorn was nowhere to be seen.

Sitting there at my kitchen table, looking down at all these Chevy Silverado pictures, I started saying to myself, 'You can't do this, Kase. You can't drive a truck that big. This is a man's truck. Made for a big, tough man. Not a little girl like you. You are kidding yourself. You're too small. You should have gotten a smaller caravan. You can't tow a 4.5-tonne caravan across Australia. You can't even tow a caravan at all! You shouldn't have even gotten a caravan. You just can't tow your whole family around the country. And you certainly can't drive a truck that big. What the fuck were you thinking?'

Tears welled up in my eyes. My whole body was filled with disappointment in myself. How could I have ever thought that I could do this.

Then my eleven-year-old daughter walked into the room. Poet saw the picture of the truck and said, 'Cool.'

Trying to hide my tears, I replied, 'Yeah, it's cool, but I'm not big or tough enough to drive a truck like that, hey?'

She looked at me, then she looked back at the truck, and then she said, with her confident and bossy foghorn, 'Mum. You're tougher than all the guys we know. You can do anything.'

I heard her. I really heard her. Maybe more than I'd heard anything in a really long time.

This little powerful sentence that Poet had said so naturally.

She actually believed. Whole-heartedly. She had no doubt in me. She had only belief. And I had taught her that belief. I had taught her to have that belief in herself. But somewhere along the way, I had lost that belief in me.

I would never have talked to Poet the way that I was talking to myself. My own little inner foghorn had gone quiet, and it took Poet's screechy inner foghorn to just tell me straight out.

A picture popped up of a beautiful, big dark-brown horse called Silverado. 'Go back,' said Poet. 'Go back, Mum. I wanna see that horse!' So I clicked back to the picture of the huge horse on the screen, and I said, 'That horse is massive, Po. Do you think you'll ever ride something that big?'

'Mum, it's my dream to ride a horse that big. Of course I will.'

I looked at her and I saw all the things she will end up doing in her life because she believes that she can do anything.

Then she skipped away, and I picked up my guitar and wrote a song straight from my old, rugged, doubtful heart to her young, strong, hopeful heart.

You are a Silverado running through the battlefield.
You are a heart made of custom blood and steel.
You are the song I've known, taking the long way home,
Making our way to the top of the world
For a Silverado girl.

Speak to yourself like a Silverado girl.

'SILVERADO GIRL'

In 2023, we did not get on a plane once for the entire year, but we still made it to 106 music, working and charity destinations all over Australia (not including all the towns we also visited along the way). With our Chevy Silverado 2500 HD, during that one year, we towed our 22-foot Kokoda Cadet 2 caravan over 76,000 kilometres, made six journeys across the Nullarbor (over 4000 kilometres each time) and visited every state in Australia multiple times (except Tassie, sorry – still working on getting the van across the water!).

We stayed in bush camps, caravan parks, campgrounds, parking bays, roadhouses, random off-grid camps in forests, on beaches and outback bushland, stayed on friends' and families' properties and made a beautiful friend in Eric, the ex-truck driver who trained me in a towing course (best money I've ever spent). We found some of nature's most beautiful swimming holes, creeks, rivers and waterfalls, and swam with crocodiles (not by choice – we found out after that they were there). My kids and I taught music in remote Aboriginal schools and shared family singalongs around campfires. I taught my kids survival skills from my childhood and how to cook on the campfire, and we made damper and pasta from scratch outside in nature.

We played board games in stormy weather, we had roadhouse showers, we visited Aboriginal communities and heard stories from their history. We fished for barra in the Northern Territory, found opal with black lights and held baby wildlife at the kangaroo orphanage in Coober Pedy. We set up loud electric guitars in the middle of the bush, hundreds of miles from towns. We caught fresh crayfish in my hometown, swam in natural hot springs and got bogged in sand dunes in Eucla, on the border between South Australia and Western Australia. Then we made the kids dig us out.

We played at huge festivals to thousands of people and did little surprise pop-up gigs in small venues. The kids joined some of my gigs, playing instruments and singing with me and my dad – three generations on stage together at the one time. We wrote songs on the long drives.

I bent up the jockey wheel because I forgot to take it off the caravan, like a dickhead, before I drove off onto the Nullarbor. I bought a new jockey wheel from an old farmer on a property nearby who randomly knew Dad from our hunting days when I was a kid.

We went horse-riding in southern Queensland, rode motorbikes on the properties of random people we'd met at Western Australian skateparks, snuck our dog Buddy into backstage dressing rooms, watched the sun rise as we drove into the Kimberley, took my songs back to the places where I wrote them and had rap battles on the drive between Camooweal and Barkly Homestead. We saw wild crocodiles, kangaroos, dingoes, emu, big boar, camels, brumbies, echidnas, buffalo, wild piglets, and snakes in our camp. I took my kids to places from my childhood. We lost all our tank water when we accidentally left the pump on and then drove down a rough dirt road and knocked our tap on. Twice.

We listened to every Living End album over and over, from start to finish, in one stint across the Nullarbor, played charity gigs and met people in remote little caravan parks who became good friends. I taught my kids to make ninja stars from tin cans and toasting forks

from dead trees and we built bike jumps in the middle of nowhere that we only used once.

We made memories. So many memories.

Living my authentic life.

Living as the parent I want to be.

Giving my kids opportunities to meet so many different people from so many different walks of life. To experience different cultures, environments, climates, beliefs, lifestyles, traditions, scenery, customs and ways of living. So that, one day, they can choose their own paths with eyes and hearts wide open.

As I slowly let go of who I thought I was supposed to be and started getting back to who I actually am, my heart filled back up.

Always take the jockey wheel off the caravan before you drive away.

Find things that make you feel grounded and then do them.

18.

I choose my own definitions

Back in the mid '90s, before my first solo album was ever released, Worm and I were sitting in a pub in Alice Springs one night on tour with the family band. While we were waiting at the bar for our half-price roast-of-the-day special counter meal, we got chatting to a local guy. He asked what I did for a job, and I said, 'I'm a singer.'

'Cool, maybe you'll be a successful singer one day and I can tell people that I met you once,' he said.

I naively replied, 'Mate, I think I'm already a successful singer!'

'Oh, sorry,' he said. 'Are you famous? What's your name?'

'Kasey, but I'm not famous at all.'

'How can you be a successful singer if I've never even heard of you?' he asked.

'Well, mate, I travel all around the country with my best mate,

Worm, singing all my songs in a band with my family. That's my job. Sounds pretty fucking successful to me.'

I hadn't even started my career yet, but I already felt like I was living a dream.

At the time, I didn't really know how poignant and important that outlook would become for me to draw back on. But, over the next thirty years of living in a world where I would constantly be told what success 'should' look like, it has certainly given me a strong view to come back to whenever the noise has got too loud.

Over my career, I've heard a lot of very influential definitions of 'success'. Most of them have been based purely on chart positions, album sales, what particular radio station will play your songs, how high the rotation is, how much money you make, how often you are on TV, how famous you are, how expensive you look, how many awards you win and of course, in more recent years, how many followers and likes you get on social media.

I have always been extremely appreciative of any of those things happening to me over the years. They have all gone on to be a helping hand in making my career what it is – and I'm definitely not giving any of them back – but if I had let this list become my *only* definition of success, I think I would have missed out on so much joy and fulfilment in so many other places and things along the way.

And I'm not sure that my creative soul would have ever been truly filled up by this one-sided definition of success, either. Especially since that list is full of outer achievements instead of inner, soul-filling experiences. I think constantly chasing someone else's definition of success would have caused (and probably did for a while) an unfillable void inside me.

If I had taken on this one-sided view, would I be looking back on some of the albums I've made and loved over the years and seen them as unsuccessful? I made an album with my dad and all the kids in our family in 2009 called *Kasey Chambers, Poppa Bill and the Little Hillbillies.* It was filled with family-friendly songs that we all wrote together and recorded in our studio. We had so many laughs and beautiful moments, and the whole project gave our whole family so many special memories. We didn't sell many copies compared to my other albums, we didn't win any awards and we didn't top any charts, but I certainly don't feel like it was unsuccessful. In fact, I think of it as way more successful than *Carnival*, which debuted at number one and sold platinum but I never felt a personal connection to. The *Little Hillbillies* album filled my heart and soul. How could that *ever* be seen as unsuccessful?

If I was always chasing numbers and statistics and nothing else, would that ever truly inspire my creativity to make the next album?

If I was busy chasing chart positions, publicity and likes, would I even notice all the other little, unexpected, beautiful but not-so-shiny things along the way?

• • •

A few years ago, I was asked by Aboriginal musician, actor and my good friend Warren Williams to come to his childhood hometown and community to play for all of his family and friends.

I had known Warren and his family since I was a little kid, and he'd shared many stories of his beautiful homeland with us during our catch-ups all over Australia, so I jumped at the chance to finally visit.

Hermannsburg/Ntaria is in central Australia, on the traditional lands of the Western Arrarnta people, and we spent our first few days there getting to know the locals. We heard incredible stories, learnt about the local history, played songs at the community school, visited the youth centre, enjoyed campfire cook-ups and connected with old friends from our early days.

Then we played a gig to all the locals and folks from neighbouring communities and outback stations. After our songs, Dad, Brando and I joined Warren and his six-piece local band for the rest of the night. For the next few hours, I played rhythm guitar and sang back-up harmonies on every old American country song I had ever heard during my childhood.

That gig wasn't a big, lucrative career move. There was no publicity attached to it, and it didn't fill up our bank accounts, but it did fill up our hearts and souls. We made some beautiful memories and some beautiful friends, shared some beautiful music, and I went away from the whole weekend feeling like it was a huge success.

Choosing my own definition of success has really made my career so much more meaningful. I don't ever lower my expectations or goals, but I do try to check in with myself regularly and make sure that my expectations and goals actually do resonate with my true definition of success – and not one from the music industry handbook.

I get to choose my own definition of success.

Sitting here now, looking back on my career, I feel successful. But that's not measured at all by how many awards I've won, my chart positions, or the followers and likes I have. Even though I am proud

of and grateful for all those things, this feeling of success really has a lot more to do with the fact that I've been able to honour my true inner creative and bring my heart songs to life. I've gotten to share them with people from all walks of life and continue my success based on inspiration and motivation, rather than on desperation to be famous or top any charts.

I've felt successful in music since before my first solo album was even released. Back then, I had already written and brought to life a bunch of beautiful songs from my heart. I'd already recorded them with some of my favourite people, and shared them live at gigs with my family all over the country. I'd met so many beautiful people while doing it, and I had faith that my higher old mate would help my album reach all the people who it was meant to reach.

I still believe that every one of my songs will find the ears that are meant to hear it. Sometimes it might be a lot of people, but other times it might only be one person and they heard that one song at exactly the right time.

I don't really need a chart or an award to tell me how successful I am.

I feel successful because my creative heart is as happy as a pig in shit.

I've had the same hairdresser for many, many years now. Jo is a sixty-three-year-old wizard. The Gandalf of Angel hair extensions. (She may have even done his too?)

I always leave the appointment feeling like a million bucks. Every single time. With a positive mindset, a full heart and a beaming smile, I walk out of the salon with the confidence and belief in myself that I haven't always felt before going in.

God forbid you ever find yourself stuck in the salon at the same time as me, though, because Jo and I do love a big, deep chat during the process. We have told each other so much about our lives over the years. Never one to sugar-coat things, Jo has shared with me her life struggles, her incredible travels all over the world, her parenting experiences helping her sister raise three kids, her heartaches and her beautiful memories. She has freely opened up to me about her journey with breast cancer in her late thirties (and approved and supported me talking about it here, of course) – she had half her breast removed, lost her hair through chemo, then went back working and travelling cancer-free for fifteen years, only to have the cancer return. She then got the rest of her breast removed, faced complications with reconstruction, and ended up getting both breasts removed. Jo battled through, and still works a full-time job, runs her own business and now helps to take care of her husband, who recently suffered from lung complications.

One day during a recent appointment, in the same breath as she told me about donating all of her real-hair wigs from her chemo days to a cancer clinic years ago, Jo also shared her lentil and vegetable soup recipe with me.

I looked up at her, saw her head full of grey hair, her flat chest from her double mastectomy, and thought to myself, *I have honestly never seen a more beautiful woman in my whole life.*

The beauty was just beaming from her.

As it did every single day.

I looked in the mirror at my half-foiled, uncoloured, unfinished hair, and – with my already full heart and beaming smile – I realised in that moment that it wasn't the end result of my hair that made me feel so good. It was Jo. It was spending time with this incredible, real woman with the most beautiful, open heart.

Being around someone whose beauty shines so brightly from within can draw out the beauty in everyone around them.

And her soup recipe is on the next page (if you were wondering).

Beauty shows up in many ways. When you let the glow of your true beauty shine from within, it draws out the beauty in everyone around you.

Hot lentil and vegetable soup

1 tablespoon olive oil
1 onion, finely chopped
1 garlic clove, finely chopped
1 carrot, finely chopped
1 celery stalk, finely chopped
2 tomatoes, finely chopped
800 g (1 lb 12 oz) tinned organic lentils, drained
400 g (14 oz) tinned organic chopped tomatoes
6 cups (1.5 litres/51 fl oz) water
2 stock cubes
1 sachet (or 1 tablespoon) tomato paste
2 bay leaves
½ cup (125 ml/4 fl oz) white-wine vinegar

Heat the oil in a saucepan with a lid, then add the onion and garlic. Cook until the onion is transparent, then add the carrot, celery and tomatoes. Just cook through, and allow the oil to coat all the vegetables – approximately 3–4 minutes.

Add the lentils, tinned tomatoes, water and stock cubes. Stir.

Bring to the boil, then turn down to a simmer, and add the tomato paste and bay leaves while stirring.

Place the lid on the saucepan and gently simmer for at least 1 hour.

Just before taking the soup off the stove, stir in the white-wine vinegar, then serve.

Enjoy xxxx

I was in my early forties, sitting in a make-up chair getting ready to walk the red carpet for the Golden Guitar Awards in Tamworth, when the make-up artist entered the room, walked straight up and welcomed me by tapping abruptly on my wrinkly forehead. 'You could definitely do with some Botox, love.'

A little wide-eyed at this questionable greeting, my inner foghorn and I simply replied, 'Nah, I don't ever need any of that. These lines tell my story.'

With every year that I get older, I'd like to think that I shed a few more layers of the things holding me back from living a full life, led by my inner foghorn. I think the simple realisation for me is that, the more that I tune into her, the less likely I am to be a dickhead. To myself and to others.

The kinder I am to myself, the kinder I can be to others.

The more truthful I am with myself, the more truthful I can be with others.

The more accepting I can be of myself, the more accepting I can be of others.

And the more authentic I am with myself, the more authentic I am with others.

I see my life as a big long gig that I'm performing with a band made up of all my authentic voices: the creative, the leader, the nurturer, the lover, the giver, the woman and the free spirit. They don't all need to sing loud and at the same time. There is no lead singer. They all support one another, and let each other take the lead when the time is right. Sometimes, the nurturer sits back and just sings back-up while the creative steps out on centre stage. Sometimes, the creative sits back and lets the free spirit do her solo. Sometimes, the free spirit steps aside and waits for the giver to lead the band for a bit.

Sometimes the voices need some beautiful harmonies from each other, and sometimes I get friends and family to join the gig when I need help.

Sometimes, the gig is heartfelt and emotional. Sometimes, it is light and easy.

Sometimes, the audience is cheering and supportive, filled with love and encouragement. Sometimes, they are distracted, all drinking at the bar or booing at me to get off the stage.

I'm trying every day to show up as the person I want to be, and also to let the gig flow as much as I can. I am trying to have enough faith in myself and to know that my band members will step up when I need them to.

But right now, it's time for a duet. From my woman and my leader.

• • •

My mum told me one day that, for many years, she felt really self-conscious about the early wrinkles she'd developed on her face. Then, she heard a song I had written for her in 2003, called 'Mother'.

Mother, mother, won't fall from grace.
Light a room with the lines on your face.
And if you were a river run dry
I'd sing you sweet by and by.

She said that she had always thought of her aging lines as such a negative thing – until she heard that one lyric. 'Light a room with the lines on your face.' Since that day, she says she has looked at her face in a completely different light. She now embraces her lines, and every time she looks in a mirror she reminds herself of the song and smiles.

I wrote that song for her for Mother's Day, and I had always seen her lines as representing her experience, her wisdom, her true beauty. She did light up a room. Every time she walked into it. She still does. I had no idea at the time I wrote it how much of a difference one line – one small, changed perspective – could make in someone's life.

There is no rule book for how to live our lives.

Everyone's journey is their own. We all have different paths, with ups and downs, twists and turns, choices and change, but we all have one common thread no matter what. We are all getting older. Every single day. Every single minute. It's inevitable. It's a shared similarity that we all have, whether we like it or not.

We are taught to fight it. We are told that it's a negative thing, and that we should resist it at all costs. We are trained to keep the battle against it alive for as long as we possibly can. We are conditioned to believe that youth equals beauty, and that aging represents losing that beauty.

But what if they are wrong?

What if they are *so* wrong that it's actually the exact opposite?

What if our true beauty lies *within* our aging experience?

What if I simply choose to not believe what I am told anymore? What if I choose to see getting older as the most beautiful and empowering thing that could ever happen to me?

Every day that I get older, I have a chance to create more memories to show on my face, to have more experiences and to learn more about myself. To strip back more of the bullshit layers, and get to know my true self and others better.

Every day that I get older, I have a chance to learn from my mistakes and my fuck-ups. I get new choices every day. I get more knowledge every day, and because of that knowledge I even sometimes make good choices.

What if we were taught that getting older is a beautiful gift?

What if we were taught to feel grateful for that beautiful gift?

What if I just decided to be grateful every day for every line that appears on my face? This obsession we have with looking younger is overshadowing the beauty we could be seeing in getting older.

Sometimes when I look in the mirror now – if I look through the eyes of my heart instead of the eyes of society – I don't just see lines. I can see every experience I've ever had. I see all the laughter and smiles. All the love that I've felt. The heartaches that I've turned into lessons. The tiring but incredible travels throughout the world. The mistakes and the triumphs. Every feeling I've had for those I've loved or lost. All right there on my face, all making up who I am.

Maybe *that* is true beauty.

And who gets to decide all this shit anyway?

I can choose my own definition of beauty.

I know I will create more lines on my face today, and more tomorrow, but I can choose to wear them proudly instead of trying to hide them away.

And yeah, I can choose to put a bit of mascara or foundation on too, if I want, but the choice will still be mine. I can take pride in how I look without giving my self-worth away to it.

When I was younger, I would look in the mirror and see faults.

Always wondering how I could make myself look better. What would make me more appealing? What would make me look thin enough, sexy enough, young enough, pretty enough? It was all because I was seeing myself through society's eyes. Not mine. Society told me I should want to look younger, thinner, prettier but it's always been up to me whether I choose those beliefs as my own.

Now, I see happiness in my mirror a lot. I see experience. I see love. I see heart. I see me.

I can even see the older woman I am yet to become, and I am so grateful it's me who gets to create her.

Getting older is a beautiful gift that we are given every single day. The only real alternative is being dead.

I have almost fifty years' worth of wrinkles on my face from all the laughter in my life. I have a bunch of grey hairs on my head, popping through from all my life experiences. My boobs hang down to my knees when I don't wear a bra from feeding my three babies.

Am I not pretty enough?
Who gives a fuck.

Don’t let dickheads turn you into a dickhead.

Epilogue

The first thing I did after writing the opening story in this book – the one about the farmer shooting at our family in the jeep while my mum was seven months pregnant with me – was to send it over to my dad to proofread.

Obviously, it was the one story in the book that I didn't have my own personal memory of, so I was just drawing on the memory of overhearing the tale when Dad recounted it. I'd heard it a few times over the years, but Dad was always quite embarrassed to share it, and still to this day he can't believe that he actually told his pregnant wife to dangerously siphon fuel into a moving car while an angry farmer shot at us. And, as I'd read over my own recap, I'd started to wonder how much of it was actually true. It seemed a bit far-fetched. Had it really happened exactly like that in real-life?

As I've said, Dad isn't really one to embellish a story too much. But it was quite possible that *my* memory of the story had blurred a little over time. Maybe I had Hollywood-ed it up a bit through the years? I mean, when I play it over in my own head, I have cast Chuck Norris as my dad and Sigourney Weaver as my mum. It wasn't out of the question that it hadn't *really* been quite the same car-chase adventure I'd built it up to be, then described in detail in my book.

'So,' I asked Dad when I called him after he'd read the first draft, 'how accurate is it?'

He laughed. 'Well, how accurate do you want it to be?'

'Yeah, OK, I guess it needs to be accurate,' I said begrudgingly. I didn't want to lose the excitement and thrill of my opening story.

'Then there's a few things you need to change,' he said. 'Firstly, it wasn't my left-hand-drive army jeep. I had two jeeps in the '70s. You must be getting mixed up with another story. The one we were in that night was a CJ-6 with a six-cylinder Rambler motor that would easily do over a hundred miles per hour. And, as for the actual story of the car chase? That's not exactly how it happened ...'

A wave of disappointment swept over me.

Then my dad said, 'I think you tamed it down a bit. The real story is *way* more full-on than you described. When I saw the farmer come screaming out of the farmhouse in his undies with a gun, I freaked out, put the pedal to the floor and took off!

'He jumped in his Holden ute and started chasing us, so I quickly turned down a gravel road, thinking I would outrun him on the corners. But our powerful six-cylinder motor started missing, and when I looked down at our fuel gauge I realised in horror that we were out of fuel. The farmer finally gained on us, got right up close, and *that's* when he started shooting. Not at all from afar. He was right behind us!

'We hadn't lost power yet, so we were still at full speed when

I stupidly screamed at your mum that the only hope of us getting away was if she climbed over two seats into the back, opened the back *door* and siphoned petrol into the tank.

'Your mum didn't half climb out a window. She dragged an entire twenty-litre jerry can of fuel all the way to the back of the jeep, opened the full-panel swinging back door – while screaming down a gravel road at 130 kilometres per hour – and held her entire pregnant body outside the car while it swerved from side to side as I drove like a complete maniac. She didn't siphon the fuel while she was inside the car. She did it all hanging on the outside of the swerving jeep, missing the bushes and trees on the side of the road by inches.

'She held the hose firmly in place, knowing our lives depended on it, and just as the jeep felt like it would finally cough and die, the engine caught a whiff of the fresh fuel and took off. With the sudden pull, I almost completely knocked your mum out of the back of the jeep, but she held on tight for her life – and yours – and clutched her way back into the fast-moving vehicle.'

He paused briefly, then added, 'I count it as the craziest, most irresponsible, biggest dickhead moment of my life. Oh, and one more thing: your mum was actually eight and a half months pregnant.'

I re-cast Tom Cruise as my dad and Angelina Jolie as my mum.

I was born two weeks later.

My definition of 'being a dickhead'

When I …

- abandon myself to please others
- give away my self-worth to society's bullshit
- talk down to myself
- don't take the jockey wheel off the caravan before driving away
- don't listen to my inner foghorn
- let anyone else choose my definitions for me
- lose sight of my own boundaries
- don't embrace change
- think that being kind means abandoning myself
- think that being strong means being an arsehole

- convince myself that it's not OK to look my age
- blame others for my own unhappiness
- live in regret
- convince myself I don't have choices
- am not grateful
- don't listen to Paul Kelly
- don't admit when I am wrong
- behave competitively in a creative field
- parent my kids based on my own shit
- judge other people
- cook with gluten-free flour and expect it to turn out like normal flour
- don't stand up for myself when it means something to me
- compare myself to others
- don't ask questions
- am not honest with myself
- forget that positive thinking leads to good shit
- forget that negative thinking leads to bad shit
- let the outer noise drown out my inner foghorn
- get my eyebrow pierced in a dodgy backyard piercing place in western New South Wales and leave it in – even when it goes all red and pus starts coming out of it – and end up in a Dubbo hospital.

Note to self:
just don't be a dickhead.

Kasey's album *Backbone*
is available now.